10 SHEFFIEL
WALK

An illustrated guide to walks with dogs around the western edge of Sheffield

Jane Bartholomew

Acknowledgements

Firstly, thanks to The Dogs for their cooperation in the creation
of this book:
Betty, Bob, Bruno, Jasper, Jess, Jim, Kipper and Ted.

Many thanks also to the dog owners:
Caroline, Chris, Dave, Liz, Lorna and Sally.

First published in the United Kingdom by
Arc Publishing and Print 2018
2nd revised printing 2019

ISBN: 978-1-906722-58-6

Disclaimer: The walking information in this book is given in good faith and is believed to be correct at the time of publication. Neither the author or the publisher accepts any responsibility for errors or omissions, or for any loss or injury howsoever caused. You alone can judge your own fitness, competence and experience and you should do so before setting out. Walking can be a hazardous activity and only you can judge the level of your own fitness and which walks are suitable for you. It is the responsibility of individuals undertaking outdoor activities to approach the activity with caution and, especially if inexperienced, to do so under supervision. The walks described in this book are not strenuous but individuals should ensure they are suitably fit and correctly dressed before embarking upon them.

Contents

Acknowledgements   2

Introduction   4

Location of all 10 Walks   6

Walk 1:   A Walk around Dale Dyke Reservoir   7

Walk 2:   A Walk in the Rivelin Valley   18

Walk 3:   A Walk around Lodge Moor   37

Walk 4:   A Walk around Wyming Brook   44

Walk 5:   A Walk around Fox Hagg   52

Walk 6:   A Walk around Redmires Reservoirs   60

Walk 7:   A Walk in the Mayfield Valley   72

Walk 8:   A Walk in the Porter Valley   82

Walk 9:   A Walk in the Limb Valley   94

Walk 10:   A Walk in Ecclesall Woods   109

Bibliography   119

Introduction

The moorland and the wooded valleys through which Sheffield's rivers and their tributaries flow provide an impressive range of settings for dog walking. The beauty of these rural surroundings has been noted by writers over many years. In the 1970s local historian Muriel Hall wrote:

'There are few industrial cities in Great Britain...blessed with such lovely, unspoilt, peaceful and natural countryside as Sheffield'.

The walks in this guide are located on the western edge of Sheffield where suburbia merges with this protected green belt of countryside. Writing in 1819, the antiquarian Joseph Hunter described the distinctive combination of moorland, woodland and river valleys as *'uneven but not mountainous'*, exhibiting instead the *'softer graces of landscape'*.

The Mayfield Valley illustrates the words of Hall and Hunter.

Hunter also remarked that *'Such a district as that in which Sheffield stands must abound in water. Where there are hills there will be streams'*. His two hundred-year-old observation is reflected in the fact that water in its various forms is an element of all ten of the walks in this guidebook. Eight are set within the so-called 'green wedges' of river valleys which slice into the suburbs while two are based around reservoirs which are fed by the streams running off the nearby moorland.

'Taking the dog for a walk' is a wonderful thing. In addition to the opportunities to exercise and socialise afforded by dog-walking, being outside and connecting with the natural world is recognised as beneficial for our general sense of wellbeing. As dog owners, we are compelled to venture outdoors every day and experience the range of seasons and associated weather. The light and greenery of the spring and summer months reward dog owners after the winter weeks of trudging along muddy paths in dark and dirty weather. However, the winter has its own attractions. The bare trees and subtle colours enable us to read the landscape and notice birds going about their activities, particularly when the breeding season beckons. In contrast, the later summer feels like a culmination of the natural year when nature pauses before the changes and activity associated with autumn get underway.

The walks featured in this guide are among the personal favourites of local dog owners and reflect the way in which we develop routes to suit our routines, personalities and interests as well as those of our dogs. These routes form 'mental maps' which are based upon personal associations with details of landscape and buildings which may go unnoticed by others. A woodland glade, a pool in a stream or a bench in a field can become a significant marker in our walks, so much so that we may invent names for these features. The process of charting our personal maps of the environment within which we walk our dogs strengthens our connections with the locality.

These walks may provide the reader with the opportunity to explore familiar places and experience the local environment in new ways. Around forty years after Hunter wrote his history of Sheffield, local writers Henry Pawson and Joseph Brailsford made a particularly pertinent observation in their *Illustrated Guide to Sheffield and Neighbourhood:*

Indeed, though of course every resident is familiar with the general character of the scenery of the neighbourhood, comparatively few of those who live in Sheffield have explored the whole of the lovely haunts, which are to be found within a very few miles of the town, so prolific has Nature been in her adornment of this locality.

As well as apprehending the familiar in new ways, it is hoped that the guide will also be a starting point for you and your dog to discover your own 'lovely haunts' and thus enjoy new connections with the outdoors.

Location of all 10 walks

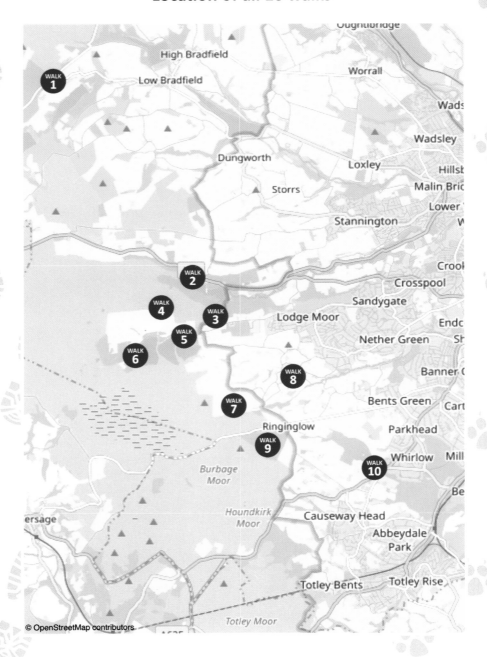

© OpenStreetMap contributors

Walk 1:   A walk around Dale Dyke reservoir

Introduction

Dale Dyke reservoir (also spelt Dale Dike) is to be found in the north-west of Sheffield, within the Peak District moors. It is one of four dams built in the mid-nineteenth century to provide water for Sheffield's growing population. As it is a reservoir which supplies the city, the land is owned and maintained by Yorkshire Water, although there are no longer the dam keepers whose job it was to ensure the dam and surrounds were kept immaculate.

This is a peaceful place for a stroll with your dog and Dale Dyke still reflects the Reverend Alfred Gatty's description from 1875 of a valley 'of singular beauty, retaining under its cultivation much of its originally wild character'. In addition to water features, the walk includes woodland and open areas. Although the paths can be very muddy after wet weather, in drier months Dale Dyke can boast a 'beach', as when the water line has receded, a sandy, stony shoreline is exposed which dogs and children can enjoy exploring. The path is designated for walkers and provides plenty of opportunities for your dog to run freely.

However, Dale Dyke has a tragic history. At 11.30pm on 11th March 1864, (just weeks after its completion), the dam wall burst and the contents of the reservoir poured down the valley to Sheffield. An eyewitness account at the nearby village of Low Bradfield describes 'a mighty wall of water running on a level with the roofs of the three-storied buildings it demolished'. Other writers described the flood as a 'boiling torrent' and a 'brown witch's broth' which swept into Sheffield 'at more than racehorse speed', flooding everything in its path. The dam emptied in 40 minutes.

From Low Bradfield to the centre of Sheffield 'stretched a broad ribbon of desolation': two hundred and forty people and hundreds of animals died while mills, cottages and buildings were wrecked.

The dam was rebuilt in 1875 in the light of lessons learned from the disaster and it currently holds 446 million imperial gallons of water.

The great Sheffield Flood continues to be remembered, in Gatty's words, as 'one of the most appalling visitations that ever befell' Sheffield.

Dale Dyke reservoir route

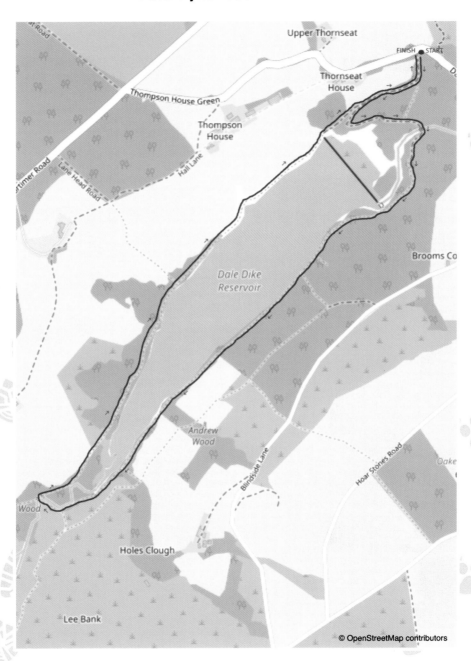

Starting point:	Dale Road
Location:	S6 6LE (nearest postcode); Grid reference: SK 23360 91875
Distance:	Approx. 2½ miles
Time:	Approx. 1½ hrs

There may be livestock and game birds in adjoining fields and water fowl nest in this area, so your dog will need managing accordingly.
There is a waste bin at the entrance to the reservoir site.

Directions

Enter the reservoir area and follow the signpost to walk down the wide, sloping path. On your left, you will soon catch sight of the view across the reservoir site and to the moors.

There is a marker in the ground on your left which signifies the original line of the dam before the disaster took place.

CLOB: Centre Line Old Bank

Take a left to follow the path downwards through an open patch of gorse and broom scrubland which is used by the water authority. The huge grassed slope of the dam wall lies behind you and ahead you will see an area of tall conifers. The sound of gushing water can be heard and you will soon reach a bridge over the Dale Dyke as it flows out of the dam and runs east to join Damflask reservoir.

The path down from the road.

Once over the bridge, follow the path right through the area of conifers and rhododendrons and you will reach some waterworks with a rather grand stone archway dated 1887, the year the dam was refilled.

Walk up the steps running alongside the works to reach a shady plateau set within tall conifers.

Then climb a mossy bank via another set of steps past rhododendrons.

At the top, follow the path right to walk along a track which is soft with a thick layer of leaf mulch. Proceed through the pines, oaks and birch with the reservoir on your right.

Scatching and sniffing amongst the leaf humus and roots.

As you proceed, on your right you'll see the dam weir and ornamented stone bridge.

Past the entrance to the bridge, you will see a further sharp-angled weir which can look beautiful in the sunlight.

A little further along the path through the wooded section, you will come across a mysterious-looking building which is owned by the water authority.

A lonely lodge.

The walk then continues along Bradfield Dale as it follows the bank of the reservoir with views across to the other side of Dale Dyke.

The plants growing here are a reminder of your proximity to open moorland: in 1819 the antiquarian Joseph Hunter described the terrain here in terms of 'a few stunted trees...fern and heath... mixed indeed with the slender wires of bilberry'.

The slender wires of whippets amongst the 'slender wires of bilberry'.

In contrast to the roar of water heard earlier, it should now be peaceful. The tranquil scene looking north west across the dam can be enjoyed from a thoughtfully-placed bench. The sounds of waterfowl may be heard and it's a beautiful sight when a flock of greylag or Canada geese come swirling across to land on the calm sheet of water. However, you may also hear shots ringing from across the valley, reflecting Joseph Hunter's remark back in the early nineteenth century that the area is 'a great scene of grouse shooting'.

The view across the reservoir to Hallfield House, which dates back to the 13th century.

The path then becomes a track bordered on one side by bracken and on the other by a stone wall which edges a conifer plantation. Continue past the opening up to the left to Roger Lane.

After around 10 minutes, you will pass another turning to the left which leads up towards Ughill. However, your path takes you past a small pond and a wooden footbridge near an area called Andrew Wood.

A family of Greylag geese.

The walk is now reaching the south west end to the dam and you will notice how the banks of the opposite shore are much closer. You may see mallards perched in amongst the trees overhanging the shallow bank.

The shore flattens out here, allowing dogs to swim or paddle, depending both on their inclination and the level of the water. Continue onto the open area of bracken at the tip of the reservoir; there is a short wooden signpost here: bear right and through the bracken.

If you wish to make a detour at this point, there is a footbridge to the left which leads up through an area called 'Brogging' to Strines reservoir.

To continue this walk, however, take a right over the wooden footbridge across the overflow water from Strines which runs down into Dale Dyke.

Follow the path which runs along the south-west-facing bank of Dale Dyke so that the reservoir is now on your right. Depending on the weather, there may be several very muddy areas to negotiate as the water runs down from the fields across the path and into the dam.

The tower of Boot's Folly at Strines Reservoir can be seen to the right.

In the summer, the water is often low enough to reveal stretches of flat, sandy 'beaches' along this stretch and it's possible to build 'sandcastles'. This is also a good spot for stone-skimming.

Canine swimmers will appreciate opportunities to retrieve sticks from the water.

It may be a cold winter's morning, but nothing stands in the way of this Labrador's desire for a dip.

This is a wooded area which borders fenced-off fields in which you may see ducks feeding. Grouse shooting takes place nearby so there may also be game birds, or their remains, in this area. If you are concerned about your dog coming across a carcass of one of the poor creatures, you may need to be vigilant around here! Additionally, in the breeding season, young ducks and geese may be present, so dogs will need to be under control.

Hmmm... looks interesting, but there's nothing in there for you whippets.

Continue along the straight path: this is bordered by trees which can be partially submerged when the dam is full. When the water is low however, the flat, sandy shore of the dam provides a great space for your dog to have a chase about.

The path continues through to an open area where you will see fields and the gardens of private residences and holiday cottages banking up to the left. There are stiles for canines and humans to pass through.

You will then meet, once again, the grassy slope of the dam wall which provides dogs with opportunities to chase around with each other, (and with their owners perhaps).

At the top of the bank, you will see a further memorial to those who died in the great Sheffield Flood of 1864. Another stile takes you through to the main path and back up to the road where the walk began.

Negotiating the stile.

Further information:
http://hallfieldhouse.co.uk/history.html

Walk 2: A walk in the Rivelin Valley

Introduction

'It would be difficult to discover anywhere a more beautiful walk than that to be found along the valley of the Rivelin'. So wrote Henry Pawson and Joseph Brailsford in their *Illustrated Guide to Sheffield and Neighbourhood* of 1862.

The River Rivelin rises in the moors north west of Sheffield and feeds into a reservoir before continuing into the suburb of Malin Bridge. On this walk you head eastwards down a section of the river valley with a possible short detour to a pub, then return upstream to join a path running along the other side.

In a column from the Sheffield Daily Telegraph of the early 1900s, a journalist gives this advice to the walker visiting Rivelin:
Let yourself go. Not in a rushing sense... Just let yourself quietly follow the natural attractions of the place. You cannot go wrong... when you get home you will be prouder than ever of the fact that you are a Sheffielder.

Over the years, the Rivelin Valley has been an inspiration for painters, writers, and poets. It is said that the Victorian art critic and artist John Ruskin, having viewed the valley, decided to set up a museum in nearby Walkley so that working people could develop their artistic skills and interests. Early last century, a community of amateur and professional painters based themselves here, producing a collection of paintings which recorded and celebrated the area.

The aptly named Henry Waterfall produced a collection of poems inspired by the 'delightful valley of the Rivelin'. One of his verses reads thus:

It is thy stream so fair I see
The highest source of joy to me –
It fills my heart to think of thee
My native Rivelin

Although the valley's aesthetic qualities may be lost on your dog, if it likes water, it will enjoy this walk as there are plenty of opportunities for paddling and swimming. The paths are for the use of those on foot and, in general, this is a walk where your dog can trot about freely, meeting and greeting other canines along the way. However, it's worth being aware that as sections of the walk lie near main roads, your dog may need extra supervision at times.

In the late nineteenth century, the poet Henry Waterfall wrote about the Rivelin's 'limpid rills' with 'their long white falling streams'.

The paths can, of course, be very muddy, and there are some stone steps and stepping stones to negotiate. However, with the exception of an optional climb up a path to a pub, the going is relatively gentle and there are many benches dotted along the trail.

The historian Mary Walton concludes her history of Sheffield by telling us that the 'age-long partnership between man and nature is the secret of Sheffield'. The Rivelin Valley trail is a beautiful illustration of this 'secret'. Like the River Porter featured in Walk 8, the river was used to provide power for the production of metal goods from the late 16th to the early 20th centuries. Consequently, the valley bears many relics of this industry and the sites of nine watermills with their associated weirs, dams and goits line this walk.

The calm beauty we admire today was once the setting for an industry where men and boys could work long hours in repetitive physical labour. The stone and metal dust they inhaled as they bent over the grinding wheels contributed to a short life expectancy for the grinders.

In 1899 Sheffield Council acquired the Rivelin Valley for the benefit of the people of Sheffield and engaged unemployed men to build the Rivelin Valley Road as a tree-lined avenue which would lead from working-class areas into the Derbyshire countryside. In spite of concerns that the road might have also been a gateway for speculative builders, subsequent threats of development were thwarted so that now, thanks to the council and to The Friends of Rivelin Valley Conservation Group, we can walk our dogs within a natural setting whilst we learn about Sheffield's industrial heritage.

Green Alkanet, a member of the Borage family. This plant favours the damp, shady areas around the dilapidated walls and buildings in the valley.

Rivelin Valley Route

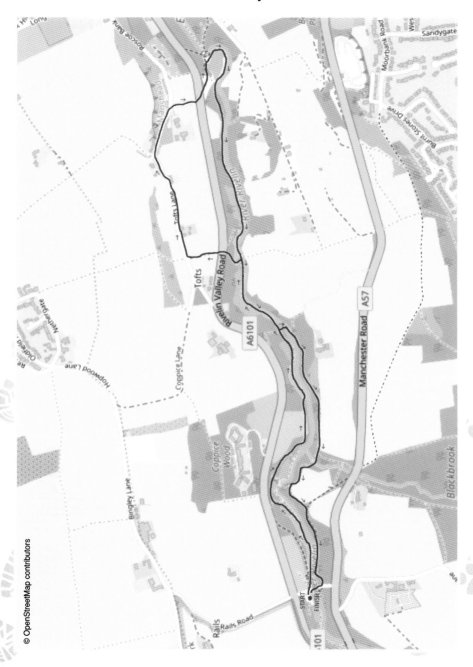

© OpenStreetMap contributors

Starting point:	Rivelin Corn Mill car park off Rails Road
Location:	S6 6GF (nearest postcode);
	Grid reference: SK 29122 87274
Distance:	Approx. 2½ miles
Time:	Approx 1½ hrs

Directions

You begin your walk on the site of a former corn mill which was particularly active during the mid-nineteenth century. There are information boards and markers here, as well as a picnic table up the slope behind the pond and a litter bin at the car park entrance.

Much has been done over the years to enhance the area for everyone's benefit: for example, here at the Corn Mill dam, there's an open air classroom area and a pond-dipping platform

Cross Rails Road to the gap in the wall and go down the steps, where you will see a field on the left where your dog can let off steam. After a few metres you will come across a stone bridge spanning the Rivelin. This is known as the Packhorse Bridge as it was used by packmen and their horses to transport goods from Crosspool to Stannington. It is a Grade II listed bridge, dating from the late 18th century and creates a very picturesque scene.

*Packhorse Bridge:
Inspiration to artists
and photographers*

*Artificial and natural water
features: goit and river.*

Do not cross the bridge but instead, take the narrow path which runs ahead of you, so that the river is on your right. You will see on your right a weir and down on your left a goit (or goyt) which runs towards a dam (or pond). Goits are channels which were constructed so that water could be fed into the dams to feed the waterwheel and then flow out again to re-join the river.

Continue along the path and, after a few minutes, you will see on your right a deep pool which can be a popular bathing spot for youngsters during the summer months. The waterfall, known as Heyden Rock is of particular interest in the way it illustrates the local geological features.

*Fascinated by the gushing water: one
of the deep pools formed by the
effects of water erosion.*

You will then reach **Upper Coppice Wheel** dam which was used in the production of knives, razors and wire.

The information board just further on gives details of the site.

Continue along the riverside path and you will reach the **Second Coppice Wheel**. To see this fully, take a detour up the little path to the left. During the 18th and 19th centuries, this site was used in the production of knives, saws, scythes and wire. More recently, The Rivelin Valley Conservation Group has done a great deal of restoration work here.

Log-balancing exercises in the rain at Second Coppice Wheel.

Follow the path back down to the riverside path, noting the remains of the mill buildings on your left:

You will now see before you a very attractive scene as the river runs wide around a bow, with a rock face to the rear. This is known as 'Cryptogam Cliff'. Cryptogams are plants without flowers and because of the moist conditions afforded by the cliff-face, examples of cryptogams such as mosses and ferns can be seen growing in abundance.

The river can be crossed here via stepping stones and then by crossing the weir. However, this can be a daunting prospect, especially when the Rivelin is in spate and the stepping stones are submerged.

A bow in the river: Cryptogam Cliff can be made out to the left.

Fortunately, there is an alternative: you can pop up the steps to the left and walk along the top of the cliff alongside the wall which lines Rivelin Valley Road.

If you do take this less challenging route, look over the wall: across the road you'll see the former King Edward VII Hospital. Now private apartments, the hospital opened in 1916 and treated patients with conditions such as tuberculosis, rickets and polio. After WW2, it became known as King Edward VII Orthopaedic Hospital before closing in 1992.

Take the steps down to the right to join the path on the other side of the river, thereby circumventing the river crossing. The view from the top of the steps down into this section of the river, with its falls, meanders and steps, is very attractive.

Cross the next short series of stepping stones and left along the pathway you will come to the site of the **Third Coppice Wheel.**

Crossing the weir. The water is brown and murky after heavy rainfall.

During the early 19th century, this became a paper mill, (it has also been known as Paper Mill Dam) and there were a significant number of buildings here, (including a tall chimney), to accommodate the needs of the mill and its workers. Leave the Third Coppice Wheel site via the steps and re-join the riverside path.

A little way further on, you will see the aqueduct across the river which used to provide clean water for the paper mill.
Follow the path over and alongside another goit.
Continue along the path and to your left an open space of grass with two oak trees in the middle opens out. This is an opportunity for your dog to enjoy the open space but be aware that the top of the field leads onto Rivelin Valley Road.

After the field, you will pass a wide weir on your right.
The water here can run strongly and quickly if it has been raining.
Walk for a stretch alongside the goit.

Then descend eight steps and pass over a little bridge which takes you over the Frank Wheel dam overflow.

You will then reach Frank Wheel dam which lies up to the left. If you take a look up at the millpond, you will see that there is a fallen tree lying across the pond which has been likened to a dinosaur.

As you continue back down to the main path, on your left you will see a stone set in the ground commemorating 10 years of the Rivelin Valley Conservation Group which continues to do much to enhance the nature trail.

The remains of buildings associated with Frank Wheel.
This site was used for cutlery grinding before becoming a paper mill in the mid-nineteenth century.

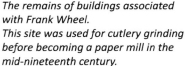

To the right there's a green metal footbridge which you'll be crossing on the way back; to the left there is a mill stone in the wall next to the path.

Next, you will arrive at **Wolf Wheel Dam**.

The mill dam of Wolf Wheel is the largest in the valley and was in use for cutlery and razor grinding from the 18th century until the 1930s.
The water wheel was 15 feet in diameter and the water from this dam powered 19 grinding troughs.

Nowadays, Wolf Wheel is home to a range of species of waterfowl and there is often a heron to be seen at the water's edge, below the overhanging trees.

The dam is popular for fishing, so beware in case your dog fancies helping itself to some bait lining the dam edge.

Walk down the steps and note the remains of Wolf Wheel's buildings which now provide a habitat for Hart's tongue ferns.

You will then reach a steep cobbled path which leads up on to Rivelin Valley Road and towards a potential pub detour.

If you choose to forgo the pub, simply continue along the path, across two green bridges and beyond past Swallow Wheel and Plonk Wheel towards Hind Wheel Dam to pick up the walk from there.

However, if you do choose to take the dog to the pub, take the cobbled path upwards and on to the road.

The path ahead if you continue on past the turning for the pub.

Cross Rivelin Valley Road and you will see some steps up to a footpath ahead of you which leads directly up between fields.

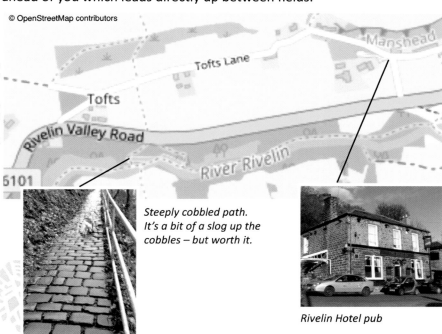

© OpenStreetMap contributors

Steeply cobbled path. It's a bit of a slog up the cobbles – but worth it.

Rivelin Hotel pub

At the top this lane, turn right and walk along the roadside of Tofts Lane which leads you through a hamlet of houses and farm buildings.

View from Tofts Lane across the valley

The footpath up to Tofts Lane.

Tofts Lane: the rocky outcrops in the centre of the picture hang behind the pub and are reminiscent of lines from Henry Waterfall's Rivelin Rhymes:

The sandstone rocks
Form many a precipice
On which the sunlight shines
That gilds with aerial gold
Its craggy creviced lines

After about 400m, you'll reach the Rivelin Hotel, which is a dog and child-friendly pub, serving fine food and ales. It has a small garden with a climbing frame at the front from which you can enjoy superb views and possibly a sunset. To the rear of the pub, there are impressive outcrops of rock, similar to the Rivelin Rocks further up the valley.

Enjoying the view at the Rivelin Hotel

To re-join the walk in the valley below, proceed down Tofts Lane. This road lies below the pub and takes you back to Rivelin Valley Road. From here, cross the road and follow the signpost which will direct you down to the left, past a grassy area with a fir tree to re-enter the Rivelin Trail at **Hind Wheel**.

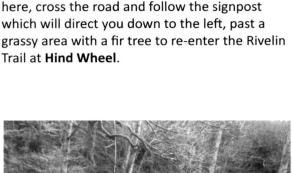

The path leading down to Hind Wheel

Hind Wheel is believed to be the earliest of the workings in the Rivelin Valley, dating from 1581. During the 19th century, this site included two waterwheels but now this landscaped area is dominated by a large, serene mill dam.

At this point, although the walk continues around Hind Wheel dam and back up the valley to your starting point, you could continue on down the valley towards Malin Bridge. This stretch of the valley includes a café, playground and children's paddling pools, as well as further examples of Sheffield's former water-powered industry.

To head back towards the starting point, walk across the green footbridge and over the head goit around Hind Wheel dam to pick up the path heading in a westerly direction.

The path then passes the remains of the **Plonk Wheel**. Once a site of cutlery grinding and possibly a saw mill, it appears to have been out of use since 1852 and there are few traces of it left.

Just beyond the next clearing are the remains of **Swallow Wheel**, named after the family of cutlers who worked their trade here during the 18th century. Although there is not much of the dam to see today, it is a haven for wildlife.

Examples of restoration work undertaken at the Swallow Wheel area by the Rivelin Valley Conservation Group

Continue along the stone path which borders the river. This is a great place for dogs to enjoy a dip as the river banks here slope gently into the water.

I'll just stay here and watch while you brave the water.

Pass over two green metal bridges and a weir.

Continue along the path you trod earlier past the path up to the road and Wolf Wheel. When you reach the gap in the wall marked by a grindstone, turn left to cross the bridge over the river.

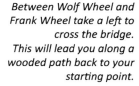

Between Wolf Wheel and Frank Wheel take a left to cross the bridge. This will lead you along a wooded path back to your starting point.

The path climbs gradually so that, in the winter especially, there are great views to be had of the other side of the valley. This vantage point provides different perspectives to the features such as the Cryptogam Cliff area noted earlier on the walk downstream.

At times the path climbs quite steeply as it skirts fenced fields on the left. Eventually, it makes a right turn at a gated field entrance. Continue along here and after about ten minutes you may be able to make out King Edward VII hospital across the valley and after that, the old aqueduct running across the river.

You will soon be able to make out the sound of traffic on the nearby A57 Manchester Road which runs parallel to this path through the wooded valley slope. At this point, you will see a track which runs steeply off to the right down a bank towards the Black Brook, a tributary to the Rivelin which you may have spotted earlier from across the valley. This stream and the surrounding area was a favourite haunt of the early nineteenth century Sheffield poet Ebenezer Elliot. His statue stands in Weston Park and depicts Elliot seated upon a favourite rock which is situated further upstream. According to Pawson and Brailsford in their 1862 Sheffield guide, Elliot's poetic sensibilities moved him to name the brook the 'Ribbledin'. Elliot was also inspired to write the poem 'Farewell to Rivelin':

Beautiful river! goldenly shining,
Where, with cistus, woodbines are twining,
Birklands around thee, mountains above thee,
Rivelin wildest! Do I not love thee.

Whether or not you and your dog choose to follow Elliot's example and spend some moments reflecting upon nature's beauty, crossing the brook may pose a challenge: although it's not wide, after heavy rainfall it can be fast flowing and too deep for walking boots. If this is the case, there are alternative paths which will take you around the top to join the footpath past the brook.

Climb up the other side of the bank and follow the path which takes you up to a wall edging a field. In the summer, the fields here are full of wild flowers.

After a short distance, the path intersects with another which leads down from the Manchester Road and at this point it widens out and slopes gently downwards towards Packhorse Bridge. Cross over the bridge and head back to cross Rails Road and to your starting point at the Corn Mill Dam car park. It's time to say 'Farewell to Rivelin'.

Further information

Shaw & Kendall's guidebook 'Walking the Rivelin' provides details of the history and wildlife of the area (see bibliography for details).

The Rivelin Valley Conservation Group's website: http://rivelinvalley.org.uk/index.php provides comprehensive information about all aspects of the Rivelin Valley.

Rivelin Valley Trail: http://rivelinvalley.org.uk/trail/wolf.php
Rivelin Hotel tel: 0114 2336650

Walk 3:   A walk around Lodge Moor

This walk contains a great deal of variety. Set on the edge of suburbia, it includes not only moorland and a nature reserve but also the sites of a former prisoner of war camp and a racecourse. There are opportunities for dogs to run freely in open spaces, explore wooded areas and dip into streams. Their owners can enjoy a dog-friendly pub, local history, ecology and spectacular views. This walk links to Walk 4 and so if you wish to extend it further along the upper Rivelin Valley and into Wyming Brook, there are connecting footpaths. During the Fox Hagg Nature Reserve sections, there are no livestock to concern you or your dog. However, there is a road to be crossed and in the middle section of this walk, there may be sheep grazing in the fields lying adjacent to the playing field and woodland.

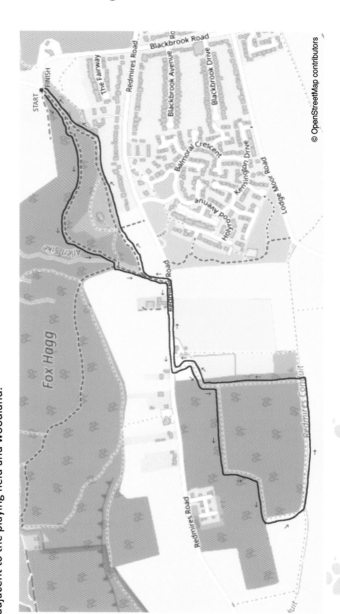

© OpenStreetMap contributors

Starting point:	Small car park off Lodge Lane: from Redmires Road head down Lodge Lane; the car park is on the left at the first steep bend in the road.
Location:	Lodge Lane S10 4LW
	Grid reference: SK 29001 86561
Distance:	Approx. 1½ miles
Time:	About 1 hour, unless you stop off in the Sportsman...

Directions

From the car park, you will see a sign showing that you are entering Fox Hagg Nature Reserve.

Take the entrance pathway on the left which will take you in a westerly direction with the city of Sheffield lying behind you. After a few metres, you will meet a 'v' in the path. Take the direction to the right, signposted as 'very narrow'. As you walk along this path, (which can be popular with mountain bikers), you will see the Rivelin Valley running along down to your right, with the pair of Rivelin Dams up ahead.

After about five minutes of walking, you'll come across a boulder in the middle of the path. Another five minutes on from this, to your left there

are outcrops of millstone grit rocks which children may enjoy climbing.

Although you are within the suburb of Lodge Moor, the path is bordered by the moorland vegetation of heather, bracken and bilberry below slender trunks of silver birch.

This is reflected in the fact that the boundary with the Peak District lies only about ¾ of a mile ahead of you.

Continuing along the winding path, after about five minutes you will come across a bench on a small plateau.

Aren't you going to sit down then?

Continue along the birch-flanked bends of the path. After about another five minutes, you will come upon the Allen Sike which leads down into the River Rivelin below. The word 'sike' is said to be a northern English term dating from the Middle Ages for a small stream or rill. Where the path crosses the stream, man-made and natural stonework, along with the vegetation combine with the water falling down the clough to create a picturesque little area.

Climb the steps up the other side of the clough and then take a sharp left up the path which will take you to Redmires Road. The road follows what used to be known as the 'Long Causey' or Causeway. This was a packhorse route between Sheffield and Hathersage and dates from the middle ages. Across the road and to your left, on the edge of a field, you will see a large red-brick building. This forms part of a private housing estate which was formerly Lodge Moor Hospital. The hospital opened in 1888 and closed in the 1990s. It was seen to be ideally placed for the treatment of infectious diseases as it was on the edge of the city and at high altitude with plenty of fresh breezes blowing in from across the moors. It was originally built at great speed in order to cope with the Sheffield smallpox epidemic of 1887-1888.

Turn your back on the former hospital and head towards The Sportsman. This dog-friendly public house serves food and has tables outside which look across the playing fields to the tree-lined ridge of Brownhills Lane.

The Sportsman on Redmires Road.

The view across Redmires Road towards Brownhills Lane.

To continue the walk, go past the Sportsman and enter the large gap in the tall stone wall which edges the roadside here. You will see before you a large car park and a continuation of the playing field adjacent to the Sportsman. This field is used by football clubs at weekends, but when it is not in use, it is an excellent spot in which your dog can chase around. Be warned, however, that there may be sheep grazing in the fields which lie beyond.

There is a wooded area to your right. Enter this from the car park and you find yourself in a very different environment which is dominated by tall pines. There is a haunting and mysterious quality to this plantation.

On the woodland floor, amongst the leaves and moss, you will see the remnants of Redmires prisoner of war camp in the form of concrete floors,

steps and foundations. Explore the area further and you will also come across the flooded remains of basements. The PoW camp was established in the First World War and one prisoner, held from 1918 to 1919 was Karl Dönitz, whom Hitler later chose as his successor to the position of Führer. During the Second World War, the camp held German and Italian prisoners and there are said to be traces of tunnels built by the few who attempted to escape.

The foundations of one of the prisoner of war buildings lying beneath the leaves.

Head west through the centre of this plantation and you will reach the edge of the trees. This looks out across fields which were once the site of a short-lived racecourse with a 'Racecourse Farm' nearby. However, from your point at the edge of the plantation, turn left and take the path as it leads you back into the edges of the wood. Follow the path running along the southern edge of the wood, with Redmires Conduit and fields running along to your right. During the late summer and early autumn, you can gather blackberries from the brambles forming the shrub layer under the trees.

Turn left so that you are following the final side of the plantation and head back towards your starting point. You may choose to cut across into the field so that your dog can enjoy some free running and you can enjoy some sunshine. Either way, walk towards the car

park with the Sportsman to its right. Cross Redmires Road and return to the opening which will take you down into the Fox Hagg reserve.

After this, the path runs behind a ribbon of back gardens, (some of which may be accessible to your dog or may contain dogs). The Victorian art critic and dog owner John Ruskin wrote that 'Sheffield is within easy reach of beautiful natural scenery' and his point is illustrated here as suburbia clearly edges against a moorland landscape. On a spring day, you may be able to hear the trilling call of a curlew from across the valley.

Wet and muddy now, looking down Redmires Road towards Lodge Moor.

Looking west towards Rivelin Dams.

You'll soon reach a very pretty juxtaposition of the suburban and the rural. There is a slope of green lawn bordered by an old dry stone wall, beyond which lie gardens. There is a sense here that they could be seaside cottages, overlooking the coast, rather than moorland and valleys.

Pampas grass standing bravely behind a dry stone wall: suburbia meets the Peak District.

At this point, follow the left fork in the path as signposted, treading down the steep but firm path bordered by a fence which also provides a welcome handrail. The path levels out to lead you back to the car park and the conclusion of your walk.

This walk provides spectacular views of the northern slopes of the Rivelin Valley.

Further information

Sheffield and Rotherham Wildlife Trust website.
http://www.wildsheffield.com/nature-reserves/our-reserves/fox-hagg
The Sportsman Inn. tel: 0114 230 1935

Walk 4:   A walk around Wyming Brook

Introduction

To those who have never visited the Wyming Brook I can only say "go". For an evening ramble or a fine Saturday afternoon nothing could be more beautiful.   Sheffield Daily Telegraph, 1907.

The Wyming Brook is a river which runs its length through the Wyming Brook Nature Reserve, (designated a Site of Special Scientific interest), in a north-easterly direction down into the lower of the Rivelin Dams. This walk firstly takes you through the brook's valley before returning via a wide pathway called Wyming Brook Drive. It sits just beyond the westernmost edge of Sheffield's suburbs and on the easternmost edge of the Peak District.

Because of its landscape of wooded slopes, mossy crags and waterfalls, Wyming Brook is also known as 'little Switzerland'. Poulson and Brailsford, in their 1862 guide to Sheffield, provide us with reasons to visit the 'wild gorge' of Wyming as 'For the student of nature or the seeker after health and mental improvement, this wild glen teems with sermons.'
Although it borders moorland where sheep graze, this walk keeps to
 enclosed trails where boulders and slopes provide a great natural environment for agile dogs and agile dog owners to explore. More sedate dogs and owners will be content to focus upon picking their way along the paths, some of which can require careful negotiation, especially when it is wet or icy. Dogs which enjoy water will literally be in their element here. As might be expected, Sundays tend to be busy, but otherwise, this is a relatively peaceful place, (apart from the sound of gushing water).
There are no waste bins.

If you are interested in bird-watching, there are many species to spot. One of particular note in this area is the crossbill. This large finch uses its cross-tipped bill to access the seeds from pine cones which are abundant hereabouts. White-throated dippers favour the fresh water habitat to be found here and can be seen foraging around the brook, with their distinctive bobbing movements.

Wyming Brook Route

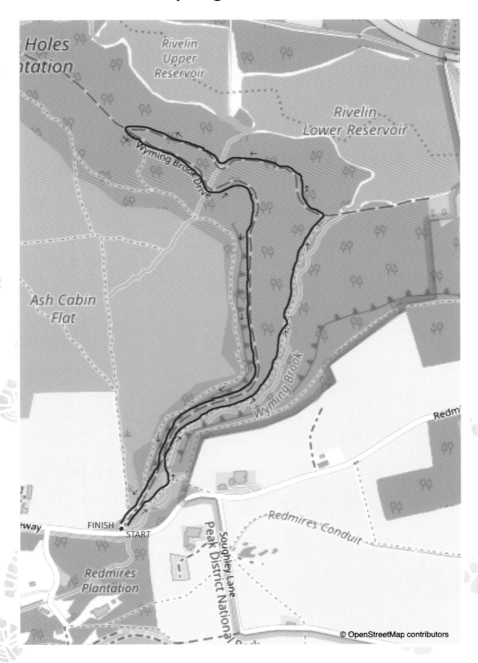

© OpenStreetMap contributors

Starting point:	Wyming Brook car park, Redmires Road
Location:	S10 4QX (nearest postcode); Grid reference: SK 26885 85823
Distance:	Approx. 1½ miles
Time:	A leisurely hour

Directions

Leave the car park to take the right-hand footpath sign-posted **'Fox Hagg'** which leads you down to the brook itself.

Cross the stepping stones, go up the steps and then take the first left along an often very muddy track which is sign-posted **'Rivelin Dams'**. To your right, there's a bench and upwards you will see the overhanging outcrops of gritstone, more of which are to be found along this walk.

View across to the other side of the valley via stepping stones.

Turn left over the first of the bridges over the brook and follow the narrow path which edges the water.

This path has a highly uneven and often muddy surface: not usually problematic for dogs, but potentially challenging for their owners.

The track continues for about half an hour, following the brook downstream towards Rivelin Dam. Along the way, the path dips, climbs, twists and turns and you will cross a further seven bridges before you reach the bottom of this section of the valley. If you look up to your left through the wooded slopes, you will see the bridle path you'll be returning along later and on the floor you may see discarded pine cones - most likely the work of squirrels.

As you descend into the valley, you gain a real sense of an enclosed gorge which is dominated by water, boulders, birch and pines. The fresh air, humidity and dappled light encourage the growth of moss and lichen over tree trunks and rocks which, together with the overhanging trees, create a primeval atmosphere.
The sound of the water gushing down from the moors dominates to the extent that after a heavy rainfall, it can be difficult to hold a conversation if you have human, as well as canine company. Waterfalls and pools are to be found at every turn, and it is worth pausing regularly to look back up the valley in order to admire the stunning views. Not surprisingly, this area attracts photographers, particularly in the autumn and after snowfall.

'Little Switzerland'

Mossy trees and boulders are to be seen throughout the walk.

Looking back up the gorge to take in the beauty: note muddy paws

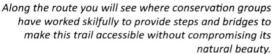

Along the route you will see where conservation groups have worked skilfully to provide steps and bridges to make this trail accessible without compromising its natural beauty.

After around 20 minutes of walking, you will leave the sound of flowing water to climb up a bank and reach a small clearing with a bench. Ahead and below is a series of wide steps which lead down to the next section of

the walk. In the wide area at the bottom here, you will find an information board, an old 'kissing gate' in the wall and a signpost.

At this point, the river runs into an underground chamber where it joins the Rivelin tunnel before flowing into the lower of the Rivelin Dams.

A right turn here will lead you to the south east corner of the upper Rivelin Dam, a car park, and another walk for another day (Walk 5, in fact).

Today, however, follow the trail to the left, passing an old gate post as the pathway begins to wind its way upwards. This wide path runs parallel to the lower Rivelin Dam which may be glimpsed through the wooded slopes to your right.

The path, which is also a bridle way, gently slopes and curves upwards. On your right is a fenced-off 'forbidden forest' of conifer woods which lead down to the western dam. There are, apparently, deer around this area, but they sensibly keep themselves safely out of the way when people are around with their dogs. Keep following the path and on your left, you will pass a bench and then see within the bracken-covered slope a small, picturesque gorge with water tumbling down from a tunnel-like entrance above. Above this, you will a higher section of the path – you will be walking along this shortly.

'Viewpoint from Wyming Brook Drive'

Keep walking up this slope for about 10 minutes until you reach the junction with Wyming Brook Drive. This is a wide, surfaced bridleway running north-south through the reserve from Manchester Road to Redmires Road. As its name suggests, Wyming Brook Drive was once more than a footpath as for a period from the early 20th century, it was used by vehicles.

In more recent times, the drive was popular with joyriders, but nowadays you will encounter only horse riders, runners and cyclists as well as fellow walkers. You will see a wooden sign post – take the direction left, sign-posted 'Car Park'. This takes a southerly direction towards your starting point on Redmires Road.

Wyming Brook Drive
It's OK – no cars coming.

Wyming Brook Drive in the early 20th Century: it looks much more like the moorland road of the nearby Snake Pass than it does today as the slopes are now wooded with mature trees.

Continue along the drive as it slopes gently upwards and follows a straight stretch. To your right, you will see wooded and bracken-covered slopes which lead up to moorland. To your left, the slopes lead downward to the path you have just climbed.

The pathway then curves round and you will see to your right the little waterfall falling down the hillside. This passes underneath the driveway and out through the opening you may have seen earlier when you were walking on the lower level of the path.

After this, the driveway curves round to the right, passing a small, wooden step ladder built into the slope. Once you have rounded the bend, another bench awaits you. This one looks north across the Rivelin Valley, and although it can be difficult to see through the tree tops, you may be able to make out the water of the Rivelin dams glinting in the sunshine.

A little way onwards from this, up and to your right are notable outcrops of rock, like those seen at the start of the walk. These seem reminiscent of the famous Easter Island 'moai' figures!

Continue along the drive and if you look down over the ivy-covered wall to your left, you will see the path you took through Wyming Brook gorge earlier.

A way marker featuring the wren: this little bird with a big voice is common to the area.

Soon on your right, you will come upon an area set back into a sheltered grassy space flanked by rocks. This has seating which has been ingeniously created by interlocking benches placed at different levels.

As you approach, you may notice numbers of birds fluttering away as the area contains a range of feeders. The bird food can also be attractive to dogs, especially if it includes fat! For this reason, I keep hold of my dog here as otherwise he will try to help himself to whatever he can find.

Local groups do much to support the wildlife and look after the area: here is a bird box.

Continuing along and looking down to your left again, you will see sights which are familiar from the outset of your walk – the first bridge you crossed, the overhanging rocks and the stepping stones. These are signs that the walk is now nearing its end.

You'll see an information board on your left and beyond that is the car park where your walk concludes.

Further information

The Sheffield and Rotherham Wildlife Trust website:
http://www.wildsheffield.com/nature-reserves/our-reserves/wyming-brook

Walk 5:   A walk around Fox Hagg

Introduction

This walk features water in its natural and artificial forms. It includes two nature reserves and begins and ends adjacent to the Rivelin Dams on the western edge of Sheffield. The route starts with a steady climb up the north-facing slopes of the Rivelin Valley and the final section follows the Wyming Brook downstream through a beautiful area which is covered in Walk 4.

Along the way, there are breath-taking views, the possibility of a visit to the pub and opportunities for your dog to explore the varied terrain. There are no sheep in the near vicinity, only horses grazing in adjacent fields at one point along the path. The trail includes a bridleway and is used by cyclists and joggers.

This is a predominantly wild and relatively undisturbed area, so as always, please be considerate to the needs of wildlife and manage your dog accordingly.

Starting point:	Lower Rivelin Dam car park
Location:	Lies between Lodge Lane S10 4LW and Redmires Road S10 4LJ (nearest postcodes) Grid reference: SK 27702 86639
Distance:	Approx. 2 miles
Time:	Approx. 1 ½ hour

Lower Rivelin Dam car park (owned by Yorkshire Water). The car park is accessed by a tarmac road running on top of the dam wall which is situated left off the A57 Manchester Road, 9 km west of Sheffield, just after the Rivelin water works. The car park is not big and can be busy at weekends - not only with dog walkers, as Rivelin Rocks across the valley is an area popular with climbers.

The 'little Gothic lodge' noted by Pawson & Brailsford in 1862 marking the turning off the Manchester Road can be made out to the right.

Fox Hagg Route

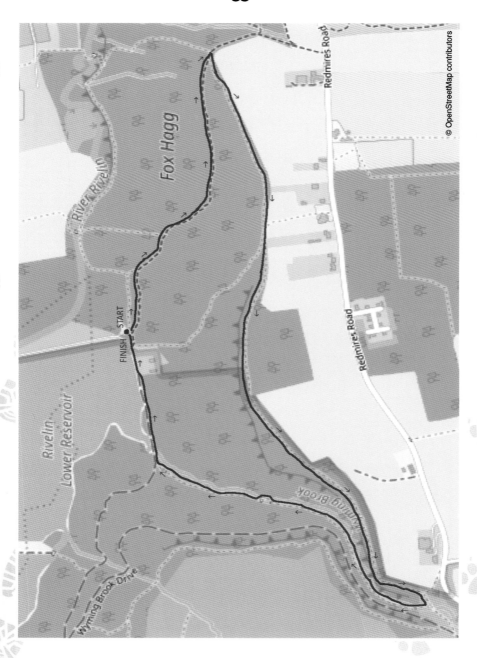

Directions

Leave the car park via the 'kissing gate' so that the wooded slopes are in front of you and the dam is to your right and behind you.

Take the path to the left and follow this as it leads you through an area which is dominated by silver birch, holly and bracken. Rhododendron bushes also border the lower slopes of this path, presumably planted here as it is not a native plant. During the autumn, the area within the birch woods to your right contains a range of fungi such as the familiar-looking red and white Fly Agaric.

Continue along the path as it begins to curve upwards to the right. On your left, you will come upon a sign indicating that you have reached Fox Hagg Nature Reserve. Follow the yellow arrow directing you onwards and upwards and you will soon reach a bank to climb. This can be challenging when muddy although at least the ascent is less treacherous than the descent.

Fungi, moss and lichen create a rich palette of colours on this silver birch trunk.

When you have reached the summit, the path opens out to the left. Following the signposts, you will pass a pair of old gate posts. These, together with the dilapidated walls and remains of stone paths, indicate former activity here. Signs of current activity are to be found in rabbit droppings along the side of the path, as well as the tracks of mountain bikes and horses' hooves.

You will reach an open area of scrubland where trees have been cleared. Half a dog!

This area would seem to have been cleared, (note the birch logs lying around) and so heather, gorse and bilberry bushes are able to grow here in these acidic and open conditions. After passing through another pair of charmingly-worn gate posts, you will see sedge growing – an indicator of the marshy ground. Perhaps this partially accounts for the name of this area: 'hagg' is said to be an old northern dialect word for 'firm spot in a bog' or 'soft spot in a moor'. Perhaps foxes frequented this spot too, (and perhaps they still do).

Soon after this, the track winds to your right and another ascent.
At the top, you will see waymarked public pathways heading in several directions.

No.342 of the Peak & Northern Footpaths Society's beautiful signs. Take the direction signed 'Wyming Brook'.

Take the stone steps up and to the right in the direction of 'Wyming Brook'. This top path runs along a line of dry stone walls and fences edging fields to your left with the dams lying below you to your right. You will be walking along this section of the trail for around 20 minutes until it turns inwards and up the Wyming Brook valley.

As you pick your way along the path, you will see on your right spectacular views of the Rivelin Valley. The Rivelin Dams, the A57 Manchester Road, the 'White House' and the moorland beyond in the west are all significant landmarks. On your side of the valley, dense silver birch and bilberry bushes cover the steep slopes.

Valley views: the road you took off the A57 lies on left side of the green triangle in the distance.

After about 10 minutes, you will see an open area of heather rising up on your left. If you take a detour up here, you will soon come upon The Three Merry Lads. The pub was named after the three Marsden brothers, Richard, George and Benjamin, who were born there in the early nineteenth century. This popular pub has a field and playground, with seating for outdoor eating, so you dog can join you for a bite to eat.

The walls with their russet colours and interlocking shapes; the stones have been skilfully selected and placed. The top is finished with a row of coping stones.

Whether or not you choose to set some time aside for a visit to the pub, the walk continues to a bench which commands a spectacular view. From this vantage point, especially when the trees are bare, the topography of the area is laid out before you, showing how the two dams sit within the surrounding natural features.

Continue along the waymarked path as it follows the line of the wall and twists, dips and climbs. Before long you will pass through an area of overhanging trees shortly before you reach the point where the path joins with the valley of Wyming Brook nature reserve. The brook runs in a north easterly direction down into the lower of the Rivelin Dams.

This section of the walk now takes you up one side of the valley in a south-westerly direction before turning back on itself to follow the stream down the other side of the valley, leading you back to Rivelin Dams.

Wyming Brook lies ahead.

Climb up to the top of the slope and follow the path with the dry stone wall to your left and the very steep slopes of Wyming Brook gorge on your right. Looking over the wall and across the fields where horses graze, you can make out Redmires Road and a high wall behind which lies a plantation: this area is covered in **Walk 3**.

This stretch of path is dominated by species of tree which are tough enough to cope with this harsh environment such as birch and larch. The gnarled, twisted and low-lying forms, whilst providing children with great climbing opportunities, are evidence of how these trees have to withstand a battering from the elements.

As you proceed, you will see on your right a large plateau of rock, covered in moss and vegetation. From this vantage point, you can see across to the other side of the valley. Depending on your inclination and agility (not to mention the weather, of course), this rock can provide a delightful place to sit and admire the surroundings. The valley does drop away steeply, however, so know your limits!

Around this point, you may be aware of the sound of rushing water. Look down through the trees to your right to catch a glimpse of Wyming Brook running below. You will soon be walking down there next to the stream.

Continue along the path until you reach a point where it slopes downwards towards Wyming Brook and joins up with some wooden steps and a wooden signpost.
Take the direction signposted right towards **'Rivelin Dams'**. Cross the bridge over Wyming Brook and proceed along the narrow, rocky path which edges the brook.

This section of the walk will take you down through the beautiful Wyming Brook gorge to Rivelin Dams and is detailed in **Walk 4**.

After around half an hour, you will reach the bottom of this little valley. Climb down some wide steps into an open area and you will meet an old 'kissing gate' in the wall, a signpost and information boards. Turn right and head down the pathway with views across the dams. Pass through the

bridle gate and you will see Fox Holes Lodge to your right. There is often drinking water thoughtfully placed here for thirsty dogs. Lower Rivelin Dam car park is ahead and your walk is at an end.

The final stretch.

View across the dam with 'The White House' visible amongst the trees.

Further information:
Sheffield and Rotherham Wildlife Trust
http://www.wildsheffield.com/reserves/fox-hagg
http://www.wildsheffield.com/nature-reserves/our-reserves/wyming-brook
The Three Merry Lads: http://www.thethreemerryladspub.com/

Walk 6:   A walk round Redmires Reservoirs

Introduction

In their guide to Sheffield of 1862, Henry Pawson and Joseph Brailsford urge the reader to take a trip 'by omnibus' to visit a '...*magnificent stretch of country, called Redmires where are situated the three vast reservoirs which supply Sheffield with water*'. This area would seem to have changed little since Pawson and Brailsford's time, with its wild, open landscape and

its views stretching across Sheffield's hills and valleys. Although only a few minutes' drive from suburbia, Redmires sits just within the Peak District National Park and this round walk passes each tier of the Redmires reservoir trio. In this 'magnificent stretch of country', dogs can run freely away from roads while their owners can enjoy a feeling of freedom on the edge of the moors.

It's worth bringing binoculars if you can, as, depending on the season, there is a range of bird species to be seen. This reflects the diverse habitats surrounding the reservoirs: woodland, moorland, farmland, marshland and wetland are all to be found in this walk. In spring, the plaintive trill of the curlew can be heard, along with the 'goback-goback' of grouse on the moors. The reservoirs also attract water fowl and waders. Greylag and Canada geese take advantage of the adjacent farmland whilst species associated with coastal habitats such as oystercatchers with their vivid orange beaks and black-headed gulls take up residence at certain times of year.

Given the birdlife and the proximity of sheep to the path at times, dogs will need managing accordingly. Apart from the provision of dog-waste bins there are no other amenities. In spite of, or maybe because of this, Redmires is a favourite of many local dog owners. It's also popular with bird watchers, walkers and cyclists and in the warmer months, for anyone just wanting to have a picnic in the countryside. In spite of the fact that its popularity brings lots of visitors, the sheer space of Redmires enables people and their dogs to be spread thinly and so a sense of peace and stillness pervades even at 'busy' weekends and holidays.

The pleasures of Redmires being enjoyed at different seasons.

The Upper, Middle and Lower reservoirs were built in 1854, 1836 and 1849 respectively as the need for clean water increased in line with the growth in Sheffield's population. Originally, the water flowed down a conduit into reservoirs which lay in the Crookes area. The water works of tunnels, pipes, channels, culverts, conduits, walls and weirs necessary for managing this natural resource are evident throughout the walk. The skilful stonework associated with these artificial features is very attractive, especially as the local gritstone used in the construction of the dams and their works has weathered in over the years. These man-made structures are complemented by the many natural formations of water to be observed: cloughs, brooks, streams and rills run down through the moorland and sedges to create the mires, ponds and puddles which develop in wet weather.

Beautiful and diverse formations of water and stonework feature in this walk.

Redmires Reservoirs Route

© OpenStreetMap contributors

Starting point:	Car park at NW corner of upper reservoir.
Location:	S10 4QZ (nearest postcode);
	Grid reference: SK 25654 85674
Distance:	Approx. 2½ miles
Time:	Approx. 1½ hours

Directions

The car park is close to the site of the Victorian 'Ocean View' pub. It would have commanded an impressive view of the upper reservoir which may have looked ocean-like after a few pints, perhaps.

Cross the car park to the left and over a small brook with a bridge across it. Turn right to cross the stone stile onto the tarmacked Redmires Road and turn left. The road links with what was known as the Long Causeway, (originally known as 'Causey' meaning road, lane or track) and this ancient road is still marked as such on some maps. Roughly up until the late eighteenth century, the Long Causeway was the route taken by packmen and their horses on their journeys across the region. Treading along what was little more than a track of flagstones, they crossed the location of the present day upper reservoir to join what is now Redmires Road and continue their descent towards town.

The Upper Reservoir seen empty: the old way-marker or 'stoop' which stood on the path of the causeway has been revealed and can be seen to the left (circled)

As the road curves round to the right, the exposed banks of upper reservoir may be seen. When the water is low, sandy shores and fissures are revealed. Apart from the bird calls, all seems calm and quiet. The dam's presence adds to the sense of stillness and, over the seasons, its mirrored surface reflects the fluctuating hues of the sky above, from slate grey to deep azure.

You'll soon reach the point where the upper and middle reservoirs meet.

For a short diversion here, cross the road over the iron bridge and enter the opening for the footpath, (which leads to the Rivelin Valley). On the left runs a culvert with an ominous-

looking drain hole set into it. To the right sits a very compact little building which is decrepit but retains a fine chimney.

Back onto the main path again, continue walking along the road for about five minutes. On the right is a conifer plantation which, when stirred by a breeze, lets out a gentle sea-like 'shh'.

On the ground to your right, you will see the old stone sign for the Victorian Grouse and Trout Inn which stood here until the 1950s. The three trout are clearly visible, but the grouse's head has long since broken off (although its little legs are still evident). Grouse shooting continues to be a

moorland sport hereabouts and you may hear the sound of distant gunshots during your walk. Under the carvings, there is a rather peculiar inscription of the words 'Ich Dien Dinner' ('I serve dinner'). The German phrase 'Ich dien' has a traditional association with honour and duty and is used to this day in royal and military emblems, (the current two pence coin bears the inscription below the Prince of Wales feathers). Perhaps the motto on the pub sign was a slightly irreverent play on this idea.

On the other side of the plantation, (which is signposted as a nature reserve with no authorised access), there are stone gateposts and a doorstep still looking out across the middle reservoir. During the building of the reservoirs, the inn was a popular watering-hole for the construction workers.

However, according to the historian Muriel Hall, the men called The Grouse and Trout the 'Eyes and Ears' because of the drunken brawls which took place there! The need to manage the level of human activity going on around the edges of the reservoirs contributed to the demise of both the Ocean View further up the road and the Grouse and Trout earlier last century. This tension between public use and the need of the water authority to carry out their remit of supplying clean water to the city of Sheffield is ongoing, as illustrated by the fencing around the footpath route, some of which is cut open by walkers in order for them to access the reservoir land freely.

The walk on the road curves parallel with the grassy banking of the middle reservoir to the right, passing water works with a weir channelling the water as it flows underground. On your left are fields of flat pasture where you may see lapwings diving around in the breeding season.
The round-winged shape of their dipping and diving flight gives them their official name whilst their piping, twirling, musical call has given them their common name of 'peewit'.

After a few minutes, dip right through a stone stile, (there's a waste bin here), and into a plantation.

Cross over the conduit running down from the reservoir and follow the path running alongside a wide channel which snakes off into a tunnel. In the summer, this secluded and still area is a mass of green from trees' foliage but throughout the year the ground is greened by soft moss which is spread thickly over the branches, trunks and undergrowth, acting like snow to muffle sounds. A primeval atmosphere is created here with the dinosaur-like trees lying at right angles, with moss hanging from their limbs.

Approaching the underground waterworks bunker.

The path soon turns right and on the left is a flat, green expanse which covers the roof of modern water works.

Walk down past the water works and at the opening to a driveway in front of you, turn right and you'll pass through an area with a number of dwellings. Walk along the driveway and before you reach the garages and vintage cars, take the walled and wire-fenced footpath which runs second left, over a small rivulet gushing down from a pipe from the lower reservoir.

Continue up the narrow path with the broken wall, miscellaneous buildings and banking to the left.

The path now borders the lower reservoir and eventually the conifers drop away and you emerge into open space with a view to Wyming Brook farm below to the left. You may see caravans pitched on the farm site.

Hole in the wall providing views north to Wyming Brook and beyond.

This potentially very muddy track is bordered by a wire fence which leads you either right to Redmires lower reservoir or to the left and Soughley Lane and the boundary line of the Peak District, (and a waste bin).

Take the former path right, through the wooden kissing gate. Behind to your left the fields rise up to the ridge and Fulwood Booth before dropping into the Mayfield Valley. Canada geese make use of these fields during the breeding season.

Never mind the scenery – what about some throwing and fetching?

The open beauty and clear air of Redmires is most evident on this section of the walk, as you skirt the southern edges of the dams, away from the road and waterworks to the north. A sense of endless sky and upland predominate and perhaps the only sound to be heard is the honking of geese. In summer months, the area is festooned with wild flowers and the reservoir surface can be Mediterranean blue. This contrasts with the steely greys of the reservoirs in winter when there's swampy mud to be negotiated. The presence of reeds growing alongside the path is a tell-tale sign of this boggy terrain which many dogs, as well as their owners, are keen to avoid.

Continue along the footpath to where there is a small gorge on your left. This is a little area of rowan trees and a wander up here can reward the dog walker with a lovely spot for a picnic. Song-birds such as the chaffinch take advantage of the habitat.

A few minutes more of walking and you will move away from the lower reservoir, climbing diagonally up through sedgy moorland to follow the track to the right. The lower reservoir lies below, but you can see the middle reservoir as a ribbon of water ahead and then the brown string of wall of the upper reservoir above that. Continue on the path which is flanked with gorse and bilberry bushes.

He's ready for some 'stones in the water'.

As you are climbing, remember to look back to the stunning views across the valleys to the north and east.

Having reached this level, you may be able to see the gentle faces of Herdwick sheep across the fencing to your left. This breed of sheep originates in the Lake District and was championed by Beatrix Potter.

Then the path strikes out diagonally again, leading you and your dog up to the middle dam.

Reservoir dog

Your dog can have fun and games at the water's edge if it's so inclined.

Continue along the ridge with the middle reservoir to your right and the upper reservoir ahead. The ridge is bisected by a fence which channels you up to the left.

The next stretch of path leads you and your dog along flagstones set between reeds and through moorland to the upper reservoir. From here you can look back across the middle and lower dams.

At the top of the flagstone path, you will reach the upper reservoir, the crest of which is fenced off. As with the first walk at Dale Dyke, a 'beach' may be exposed here, the receding reservoir revealing rocks which have

been sculpted by the water. This provides another opportunity for your dog to perhaps discover its 'inner poodle' and indulge in water-based activities at the fringe of the dam, (but beware of sticky mud!).

You may wish to take in the serenity of Redmires here on the stony banks. In the distance, birds call and lone figures stroll through the heather. Beneath the still water lie a ruined smithy and a post marking the line of the Long Causeway.

The large sandstone rocks are reminiscent of a Martian landscape.

The shapes, patterns and colours of the reservoir wall.

Return to the footpath and follow the track as it runs parallel with the reservoir. Keep going straight ahead over the undulating ground towards open, exposed moorland. On the left, Fairthorn Clough runs down through a gap in the sedge. This is one of the small streams from the Hallam Moors which feed the reservoirs.

Fairthorn Clough

The path snakes through the bracken around the south bank of the reservoir.

Make your way across the final stretch of bracken and through the final stile. Up to the left there's a wide track. This is the continuation of the Long Causeway rising out from the south west corner of the upper dam which was submerged when the reservoir was built. The partially paved route can still be followed up onto the moors to Stanedge Pole and then onto Stanage Edge.

Ocean view? From this angle on a winter's day, the scene can resemble one of a river estuary running into the sea.

However, the latter stage of this walk lies to the right and back up the road to the car park. As you make your way along the road, you will pass the gated entrance to Fairthorn Lodge and the driveway up to Stanedge Lodge which, like the two pubs, dates from the mid-nineteenth century and is reputed to have been used as a hunting lodge. Continue along the road to reach the car park and your journey home.

The final stretch of road includes examples of contemporary carvings and stonework as well as traditional stone walling.

Walk 7: A walk in the Mayfield Valley

Introduction

In 1819 Joseph Hunter wrote of the *'short but beautiful course'* of the River Porter. This walk begins by following the Porter's journey upstream through its steep narrow valley known as the Porter Clough. Both the Mayfield and the Porter Brooks rise near Fulwood Head. However, the Mayfield flows through a less dramatic and gentler valley than its neighbour to the south, quietly joining the Porter in a secluded area just upstream of Carr Bridge.

The name of the countryside west of the bridge on Woodcliffe can be a source of confusion and even heated debate. However, the title of this walk has been chosen to reflect a local interpretation of the Mayfield area. Although the Mayfield Brook is a tributary to the Porter, the general area west from Carr Bridge tends to be known locally as the Mayfield Valley and the names of houses, farms and roads reflect this. Apparently, there was also at one time a 'May Green' in the area which was a field used for May Day celebrations. The creamy white blossom of the hawthorn, (which grows in abundance in the valley), is called 'may' due to its flowering period, (it's the only British plant named after the month in which it blooms). Maybe this accounts for the moniker.

Local historian Muriel Hall wrote with great warmth about the Mayfield Valley:

...on an ordinary day one can wander through this little valley for an hour or more in peace and quiet, seeing little of habitation except for farmhouse or cottage and meeting few, if any, people. It is, without doubt, a treasured corner - a magic valley which must be preserved forever in its present natural beauty.

The writer would be reassured to know that these qualities remain intact and are as applicable today as they were when written in the 1970s.

Walk 7 includes a dog-friendly pub, cafés and magnificent views with plenty of benches en route. Most of the going is easy but there is a gentle and steady uphill climb with one steep downhill stretch. Although there may be livestock in fenced off fields along the way, the walk provides opportunities for your dog to trot around and enjoy a spot of ball fetching or swimming in the brook.

Mayfield Valley Route

© OpenStreetMap contributors

Starting point:	Forge Dam: small parking area at very bottom of Brookhouse Hill.
Location:	S10 4GN (nearest postcode); Grid reference: SK 30401 84949
Distance:	Approx. 3 miles
Time:	Approx. 1½ hours

Directions:

Start from the parking area at bottom of Brookhouse Hill between the signpost and waste bin. Head in the direction of 'Public Bridleway' which takes you over the little brook. According to local historians, during the late 18th century the cottages up to the left, (now called 'Beech Dene' but previously named 'Forge Cottages' and 'Porter House Cottages'), were once used as a site for the production of buttons made of Thomas Boulsover's invention of Sheffield plate. The men who worked here also lived in the buildings.

Continue up through the gateway and up the bridle path.

When the path reaches the open field, follow the sign pointing down to the right. As well as horse riders, the path is popular with joggers and cyclists and there may be sheep or cattle grazing on the sloping field to the left. Walk west down the bridle path. Ahead lie what in 1819, James Hunter described as the 'softer graces of landscape'.

Cross Woodcliffe Road and take the middle opening which leads into a field (which is good for blackberrying).

A winter's afternoon: the splendour of the setting sun as it begins to sink towards the west

Take a right tangent across the field towards the signpost which points you onto the footpath of the Sheffield Round Walk. Follow the right hand path down over the first of many small bridges and you may now be aware of the sound of the brook as it babbles over rocks and stones. At this point, across marshy ground to the right, lies the confluence of the Mayfield and Porter Brooks.

Follow the riverside path round to the left. You may notice a spot where the orangey-brown iron ore deposits run into the course of the river. On your right is a field where sedge grows, a sign of the marshy ground. There are often cattle grazing on this land in the summer months.

Continue along this stretch, passing another bridge and benches which are ideally placed to capitalise on this particularly lovely spot. In the spring, snowdrops and then daffodils grow in the grass here and chaffinches, robins and great tits can be heard.

After a few minutes, you will reach an opening in a wall and the junction of Mark Lane, (possibly named after a man who lived nearby) and Clough Lane.

At this 'mini roundabout', take the Clough Lane exit, which leads straight ahead up towards Porter Clough. Cars, (and motor bikes), do occasionally travel along Mark Lane, as do cyclists and horse riders and so on Sundays in particular, it can be a surprisingly busy little junction.
Continue along the rough path for a few metres before entering through an opening in the wall to your right.

As you've crossed the Porter once again, it's now on your right. Proceed upstream for about 100m, (there may be sheep in the field on the other side of the river), and you will become aware of the increasing sound of rushing water. You will then meet with a scene which Pawson and Brailsford in their guide from 1862 described as:

...one of the most perfect cascades a lover of nature could wish to see. It is in a small glen, a little way from the road, and unknown, even to many who live very near. The water falls some fifteen feet, and in a charming variety of forms.

After you and your dog have taken your fill of this picturesque scene, continue up the path and you'll come across another beautiful little area around 'Oliver's Bridge' which was named after a member of Friends of the Porter Valley organisation which does so much to preserve and enhance the area.

Looking back across the field and up the other side of the valley, you may be able to spot two major residences which date back several hundred years: Bennet Grange is situated to the left and Fullwood Hall to the right. The Fullwood Hall we see today dates from the early seventeenth century at a time when it was owned by the Fox family. George Fox, or 'Fox of Fullwood', (as the historian Joseph Hunter referred to him just over a century later), is infamous for taking the 'low road to ruin', squandering the family fortune and subsequently losing the estate.

Oliver's Bridge

You will then reach the next junction with Clough Lane. Follow the sign for the Sheffield Round Walk which takes you up Porter Clough. The next section of the walk illustrates Joseph Hunter's two hundred year-old description of Sheffield's 'Close and well-wooded valleys, with streams glittering along them...'

The field to the left drops down to the brook very steeply with tracks formed by cows cut into the grassy slope. Your gently uphill path runs in parallel with the Porter.

The 'magical' quality of the Mayfield Valley is truly evident here. This dramatic and shady environment is dominated by huge beech trees and the diagonals made by the slopes and dry stone walls. Small waterfalls and rivulets run down the steep banks while the sound of gushing water can be heard as the stream meanders along its descent.

While you admire what's ahead, remember to look back at the stunning views down the valley towards the city. You may be able to pick out landmarks such as Mayfield Heights, Whiteley Woods Apartments, the Royal Hallamshire Hospital, the University Arts Tower and buildings within the city centre.

As your ascent up the clough continues, larch will begin to take over the slopes to your left. After a heavy rainfall, dozens of rivulets run off from the sodden fields to both sides and there is a powerful sense of water moving throughout the valley.

Ten minutes or so later, you will meet a series of three footbridges spanning the Porter. Fulwood Lane and the source of the Porter lie ahead but instead follow the path to the left as it twists and turns to reach the top where there is a small bench.

Here, the opposite side of the valley flattens out into an area where there are more beech trees. Be aware that this area leads onto a road which borders sheep fields. Past the huge beech there is a car park with picnic benches.

Turn left onto Fulwood Lane and proceed along the gulley which acts as path alongside the road. On the left is a line of tall trees edging the stone wall. A gap in the trees here provides another marvellous view. The wooded Porter Valley can be traced, with the pale spire of Ranmoor Church just beyond. Further ahead to the east and beyond the city centre is Rotherham.

At this point, you could make a detour to visit Mayfield Alpaca Farm. As well as the animals to see in the park, there is a café with an outdoor eating area. Dogs are welcome provided they are under close supervision.

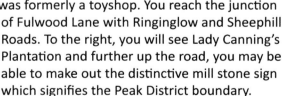

To continue the walk, pass through the village of Ringinglow with its interesting mixture of buildings which include stone cottages, converted stables and a 'Toy Cottage' which was formerly a toyshop. You reach the junction of Fulwood Lane with Ringinglow and Sheephill Roads. To the right, you will see Lady Canning's Plantation and further up the road, you may be able to make out the distinctive mill stone sign which signifies the Peak District boundary.

Walking in an easterly direction with the afternoon sun on your back.

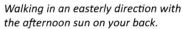

Head left down the road for a few metres and you'll see the eighteenth century Roundhouse on the opposite corner. At this point, you and your dog may wish to take advantage of your proximity to the Norfolk Arms Hotel. This former coaching inn was built in the mid-nineteenth century. Enter at the front of the building by the dog-friendly entrance to the left. The Norfolk Arms serves food and there is an outdoor seating to the front or you can sit in a grassy area to the rear which overlooks the Mayfield Valley.

To continue the walk, follow Ringlinglow Road with the Limb Valley to your right and Fulwood to your left. After a few metres, climb over the stile into the field to take you down into the valley once again. As

the signs indicate, there are usually livestock in the fields either side of the narrow path: the curious alpacas may bob their heads up from grazing to a take look at you, (your dog will probably be concealed by the wall).

Ahead to the north lies the opposite side of the Mayfield valley. The Porter is running from west to east.

From here there are more beautiful views north across the valley. Bennet Grange can be seen in its south-facing sheltered copse and the tower of the former Lodge Moor hospital is just visible.

At the end of the path, pass through the small weighted gate and head over the next stone stile into a steep field known as 'Jacob's Ladder'. There are a number of Jacob's Ladders around the country - the next nearest being in Edale. Apparently, these hills with their steep 'stairways to heaven' are named after the original Jacob's Ladder from the Book of Genesis. When there's snow on the ground, this is popular spot for the more daring tobogganists, (less daring tobogganists are catered for on the slopes around Forge Dam) and during the 1960s, a local skiing club made use of the slope, setting up a tow-rope to pull the skiers back up the hill.

View from the top of Jacob's Ladder

Make your descent of this steep slope with its stunning views down the valley to the city and at the bottom, cross over a stile to join Clough Lane. Follow the lane down the valley, with the Porter on your left. This path runs parallel with the one you walked earlier.

After about ten minutes, you join the junction with Mark Lane and the path becomes tarmacked.

Leave Clough Lane via the signpost to the left. Follow the footpath to the left to exit this stretch across Woodcliffe Road via Carr Bridge.

Commerative stone at the opening onto Woodcliffe Road; the inscription reads : City of Sheffield This stone records that the portion of the round walk from here through Porter Clough and Ringinglow to Ryecroft Glen some four miles in extent was a gift to the city by the J.G. Graves Trust.

The name given to this bridge is probably derived from an old Norse word which refers to low-lying woods bordering streams and rivers.

Dip under or walk around the rail and continue along the path with the Porter to your left and the bridle path you trod earlier to your right.

This is a beautiful and often quite secluded little stretch, with many meanders and areas for paddling. Often, the only sounds to be heard are birdsong and the gurgling of the brook as it tumbles over its bed of stones.

After about 10 minutes, you'll reach a dip in the path. At this point, take the right fork which takes you up onto Carr Bridge path. The pond is overlooked on the left with view of the café and a grassed area.

Forge Dam café with the former dam and current pond to the left. The banking leads down to a grassy space which was once the site of another dam.

As you reach the end of Carr Bridge Path, look out for the commemorative stone on your left.

Carr Bridge Path soon meets with the bridle path. At the green railings, turn left and down the cobbled slope to find at the bottom the beginning and end of your walk.

Further information:
Forge Dam café: https://www.forgedamcafe.co.uk/
Friends of the Porter valley website: http://www.fopv.org.uk/Menu.htm
Mayfield Alpacas: http://www.mayfieldalpacas.com/index.html
Norfolk Arms Hotel: http://www.norfolkarms.com/

Walk 8:   A walk in the Porter Valley

Introduction

A guide written in 1862 tells of Sheffield's 'delightful combination of hill and valley, wood and stream'. Set in the Porter Valley, this walk shows that over 150 years later this remark remains true.

Where the previous walk followed the Porter upstream, this round walk takes you downstream for about two miles from Forge Dam to Bingham Park, before returning to your starting point. It is said that the Porter Brook is so called because its brownish colour, (which is due to iron-ore), is similar to the colour of the strong, dark variety of 'porter' beer and examples of this discoloured water can be seen along the route.

This small river has been described as now being in its 'retirement' years as formerly the Porter played an essential role in Sheffield's cutlery industry. This particular stretch was used intensively, as it powered around twenty water wheels at one time. A local journalist writing in the early 1900s described it thus:
The cutlers have gone, but their grinding wheels remain. Here in a rough and ready way they harnessed the little Porter and made it turn their wheels to grind their steel into knives.

In the early nineteenth century local historian Joseph Hunter viewed these industrial relics as 'agreeable and harmonious' within their valley setting. This is still the case today with what remains to remind us of the river's hard-working past.

The sections running through Forge Dam, Whiteley Woods and Bingham Park are part of the Sheffield Round Walk, which was completed soon after the Second World War. The Sheffield benefactor J. G. Graves valued public open spaces and it is thanks to him and the trust that was set up in his name that we are now able to enjoy this walk, as well as several others in this guide.

The walk includes a café and a playground as well as historical and natural features. *The Friends of the Porter Valley* website provides information about the historical, geographical, ecological and recreational aspects to this particular 'green corridor' of Sheffield.

Porter Valley Route

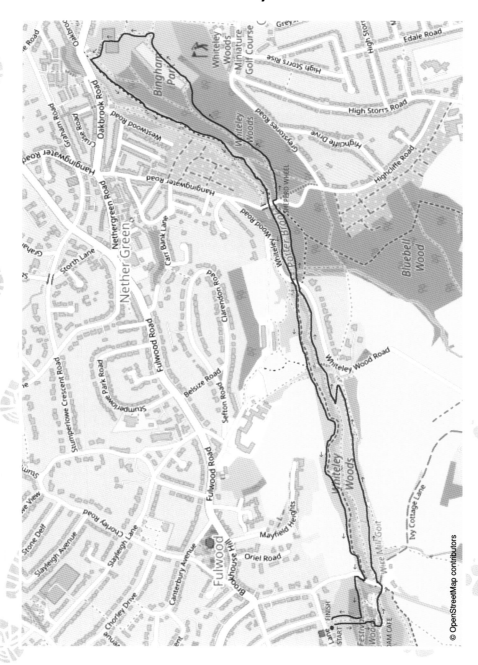

There are both relatively quiet stretches off the beaten track where you are unlikely to meet more than a few fellow dog walkers as well as 'busier' sections which are popular with families, cyclists and joggers. The route also follows bridle paths so you may encounter horses. Waste bins are situated at both ends of the walk and there are public toilets at Forge Dam café.

Starting point:	Whiteley Lane, opposite Fulwood Old Chapel (you can park on the road here, alongside the park railings)
Location:	S10 4GL (nearest postcode); Grid reference: SK 30247 85128
Distance:	Approx. 3 miles
Time:	Approx. 2 hours

Before you set off, it is worth taking note of Fulwood Old Chapel which dates from 1728. In the garden at the front you will find village stocks.

Directions:

Leaving the Chapel, cross Whiteley Lane. Apparently, this area covers an old burial ground which was in use before the chapel was built and local historian Muriel Hall's collection of local reminiscences includes a story about a ghost being seen here one night. Enter the park gate into an area known as Fulwood Green, which was once a quarry. There is a pair of trees flanking you: on the right is a wingnut whilst the black walnut on your left was planted by local musician Richard Hawley in December 2012. The fields on either side of the path provide your dog with the opportunity to let off some steam at the outset of your walk.
Head down the path through the trees. The footpath to your right leads up through the 'Festival Woodlands', planted in 1951 as part of the Festival of Britain.

Continue down the steep cobbled path which leads to Forge Dam pond.

At the bottom of the cobbled path, take a look through the railings on the left behind the litter bin: this space housed the water wheel which was integral to the original forge and dam. From the late 18th century, the pond and surrounds formed a rolling mill complex which was developed by local cutler and inventor Thomas Boulsover. Apparently, Boulsover originally tried to produce paper here, but because of the ochre mentioned earlier, the water was unsuitable. The site instead focused on the production of Boulsover's invention of

Sheffield Plate, which was used in the manufacture of buttons. After the forge ceased production in the later 19th century, the dam was used as a boating lake.

However, over the years, the dam (or pond) became heavily silted and thus unsuitable for boating. The natural world has taken advantage of this situation and so now the millpond is home to mallards, moorhen and other water fowl. 'Friends of the Porter Valley' working with the council and with other local organisations, are bringing about improvements to this area as part of an ongoing restoration project.

Turn left down the slope: here you will find Forge Dam café, toilets and a playground. The café, dating back to the 1930s, is situated on the site of the old forge and is remembered in the Pulp song 'Wickerman'. In front of the café,

an open, grassy area opens out next to Whiteley Wood Forge weir: this sunken area was once the site of a dam.

Continuing the walk, follow the path past the cottage, garages and playground to cross the Porter. If you look up, you will see a rookery in the tall trees and during the breeding season the treetops are full of activity and very noisy!

Entrance to Whiteley Woods

Follow the path down, (another waste bin is to your left), and take the second path on the right signposted 'Public Footpath' and 'Easy Going Trail'. This flat, straight stretch of path runs parallel to Wire Mill goit with the Porter Brook running down through the valley on your left.

After about 50 metres, this tarmac path combines with another one running next to fields which often contain sheep.

Continue along this top path and you will reach Wire Mill Dam, (also known as Whiteley Wood Rolling Mill). Like Forge Dam, this mill began as part of Thomas Boulsover's 'empire', producing thin steel plate and then wire over a period of around 150 years. This is a popular spot for fishing, and not only with humans: if you're lucky, you may spot a kingfisher darting in and out of the water, or herons which frequent the Porter Valley.

A goit is a conduit for water to run in and out of dams

Return to the main path to an area which used to be known as 'Bowser Bottom'. Here you'll find a more recent and formal reminder of its local inventor and business man in the form of a monument to Boulsover. The monument was erected in 1929 and assembled from a combination of remnants of the mill which stood nearby and from the hall in which Boulsover lived which stood higher up the valley. The carved elephant's head is a symbol of the Cutlers' Company.

This path continues out onto Whiteley Woods Road, (there are no barriers between the path and this road so beware from a dog point of view). However, just before the row of three 18th century cottages, take the slope which veers sharply left back and down towards the Porter Brook. At the bottom of this slope, turn right so that you continue to follow the brook downstream towards the city. If your dog enjoys the water, it will appreciate the Porter running alongside you to the left.

After about 250 metres, you will meet a metal stile.

Walk ahead, cross Whiteley Woods Road, staying on the path to the right of the river into a relatively short stretch of path which is sign-posted 'Easy Going Trail'.

Soon after entering, you will see on your right a small brook which is coloured orangey-brown by iron ore deposits. This runs down into the Porter to your left.

The woods up to your right are known locally as the Bluebell Woods and connect with fields and further woodland tracks which lead up to the suburb of Bents Green.

After continuing along the path, you will soon reach the opening where Highcliffe Road becomes Hangingwater Road. On your right, Highcliffe Road descends steeply to the bottom of the valley to where the Porter runs under Hangingwater Road which continues up to your left.

There are three entrances to this section of the Porter Valley: you are taking the one furthest to the right. Take a sharp right turn up past the

safety railings and dip left into the gap to follow the track leading up into the next section of Whiteley woods. This can be very muddy and slippery! However, once you have reached the flat stretch of path things should improve underfoot.

Directly across the valley at your level you may be able to make out Hangingwater Road with houses rising above and Hangingwater allotments spread out below. These signs of suburbia are reminders that the city centre lies only about 3 miles ahead. If you look down to your left, you may be able to make out cyclists and fellow dog walkers. The path itself runs at this elevated level through woodland of sycamore, oak and elder with a shrub layer of brambles and ivy and is relatively undisturbed. Because of this, there is usually plenty of birdlife to note. In addition to the wrens and robins, this can be a good spot to hear greater spotted woodpeckers – either their call or their more familiar drumming in the breeding season. In the winter, you may be lucky enough to come upon a flock of redwing visiting from Scandinavia. There is much for dogs to enjoy here too, such as the squirrels scampering around the trees.

5-10 minutes further on, the path takes you around a bend: after some stone stairs on your right, you will see a gap in the trees and a ramshackle kind of track, (muddy in the winter). Below the trees, in amongst the undergrowth of brambles and ivy to your right, you also will see large stones lying around and the dilapidated dry stone walls to which they once belonged. Climb the track as it veers to the right towards the metal fencing. Follow this up past the Astroturf football pitch and onto the path which lies between this and the bottom of the sloping field.

You are now in Bingham Park. The parkland was gifted to Sheffield by Sir John Bingham and his wife, Lady Maria, in 1911. Sir John made his fortune in the electroplating and silver industries and lived in Ranmoor, which is the suburb you'll soon be able to see across the valley. According to local legend, the park came about because of Lady Maria's benevolence. She could see the green 'jewel' of hillside from her garden and chose to have it given as a gift to the children of Sheffield rather than be given a gift of jewellery by her husband.

As you will see from the football pitch and the tennis courts running along to your left, this park can be used for a range of recreational activities: as well as the courts there are bowling greens which are home to an active local bowls club. Dog-owners find the former useful for obedience training and the grassy bank is a very pleasant spot on a sunny day.

This section of Bingham Park provides opportunities for your dog to chase balls, squirrels or other dogs. There's a kind of artificial spring of water in the middle of the field, (a reminder of former days when this may have been a drinking fountain), which is handy for thirsty dogs.

Continue until you meet a steep path running at right angles with path. If you walk up to your right, you could take advantage of the bench to enjoy the stunning views across the valley west to the suburbs of Ranmoor with Crosspool above.

Looking in an easterly direction towards the city centre, Sheffield University's Arts Tower and the Royal Hallamshire Hospital are prominent

features. The vista enables you to see mature trees populating the valleyside in front of you, with modern apartments amongst Victorian and Edwardian villas. St John's Church at Ranmoor is particularly noticeable with its fine, pale steeple: Sir John and Lady Bingham lived close by.

From the bench, the path running up behind you will lead you to more open space, (popular for sledging), which opens onto Bingham Park Road in the suburb of Greystones. If you look from the bench to your right, you will see a densely wooded area and, at the bottom of this, runs a stone wall which forms a boundary for Wragby Road and Rustlings Road allotments. This sloping area of woodland is a pleasant patch for you and your dog to explore, however, beware of your proximity to roads.

Ahead of you, from the vantage point of the bench, the path leads steeply down on your right towards the entrance of Bingham Park. Follow this down past the bowling greens to arrive at the wide steps which take you to the rather grand entrance to Bingham with its wide driveway and attractive park lodge. You need to turn your back on the park house to face up the Porter Valley as this is where the walk turns west towards its starting point, leaving the river to continue on its journey to the city centre to join

the River Sheaf. From this point up to Forge Dam, the walk follows part of the Sheffield Round Walk and it is easy-going and mostly flat.

This path takes you along the bottom of Bingham Park for about half a mile. It runs parallel with a cycle lane and is popular with joggers as well as walkers. You will pass rhododendron bushes to your left and then a hut on your right. Further along on your right you will see a bridge over the Porter. A waste bin is situated here.

Behind this and up a bank is the former dam for Ibbotson Wheel, named after its tenant who leased the land from 1775. It is now home to Canada geese as well as other water fowl. Continuing along the main path, the Porter Brook runs to your right.

It is generally shallow along this stretch and can be enjoyed by dogs and children. If you look up the steep and wooded slopes to your left, you may be able to pick out the top path you trod earlier.

After about 10 minutes you will arrive at The Shepherd Wheel, named after one of the mid-eighteenth century tenants of the site. This is a major example of Sheffield's industrial heritage.

Cross the little bridge to the right which leads to the workshop entrance. Inside you can see a water-powered grinding workshop. Until as recently as the 1930s, skilled grinders worked here at their 'troughs' to produce fine, sharp cutting edges for cutlery. To the rear of the building lies the restored working waterwheel.

To continue with the walk, go past the front of the building, then past the sluices and continue up to the mill dam at the top. Continue alongside the dam until you reach the opening to cross Hangingwater Road over the grade II listed bridge.

Cross the road and head into the next section of Whiteley Woods, which you passed through earlier, but this time the Porter is on your left.

As you'll see from the signpost at the opening to this stretch of the Porter Valley, this continues along the Sheffield Round Walk trail.

This area was once the site of Leather Wheel Dam. Although the dam is silted and overgrown, the path runs alongside Leather Wheel goit which used to serve the dam. Within a few minutes you will find the Porter running wide and shallow down the weir. The bridge in front of you,

where Whiteley Wood Road bisects the River Porter, is known as 'The Armchair Bridge' because a 'commodious armchair' has been built into each end of each wall.

Cross Whiteley Woods Road and enter the woods once again, but this time keeping to the right hand path which begins with stepping-stones across the

Porter. If the stepping-stones look uninviting, you can avoid them by taking a detour right and over another little bridge and stile: this takes you round to the left so that you emerge on the path with the stepping-stones behind you.

Option a) Stepping stones   *Option b) Path to the right*

You're now on the wooded path running parallel to the one you've just walked. This gentle walk which takes you west and back up the Porter Valley is part of Sheffield Round Walk and is also known also as The Whiteley Woods Trail and The Porter Valley Trail. It is a bridle path and cycleway, and so, although there are no livestock grazing in adjacent fields, there may be horses and cyclists.

This section of the Porter Valley, with its meanders and banks, provides plenty to note in terms of flora and fauna. In the spring, you may notice a culinary scent emanating from the white-flowered wild garlic which grows in profusion on the broader banks of the Porter. There is a range of birdlife to look and listen out for: you may spot grey wagtails, (which are yellow as well as grey), bobbing around in the shallows of the Porter as well as herons.

Although we're in woodland, we're also in suburbia. As the woodland path climbs and dips, you will see that there is an opening on your right through a metal stile: this path leads up to private housing and an NHS centre, joining with Fulwood Road.

As you continue onwards, if you look up through the trees to the sloping fields on your right, you may be able to make out the buildings of Mayfield Heights (although perhaps they should be called 'Porter Heights'). Once a hospital complex, these are now private apartments and dwellings. Further along, past the area of Goole Green, there are fields where horses graze.

This section of the walk through Whiteley Woods is beautiful in every season. In addition to your dog's appreciation of the environment and the opportunity to meet and greet fellow canines, there is always some aspect of nature to enjoy. The sights and sounds of jays, wrens and chaffinches, the oaks and beeches with their ever-changing foliage or the brook itself as it flows downstream to your left are all an added bonus for dog walkers here – even in the depths of winter.

The Porter Valley is one of Sheffield's 'Green corridors':

Continuing along this woodland path, you will eventually arrive at the entrance to Whiteley Woods. When you reach this gap in the stone wall cross the road, (which is actually the bottom end of Brookhouse Hill), and enter through the stone wall up into Forge Dam Park.

On your right is a stone carved to commemorate the 'Forge Valley Footpath'. Continue up the wide steps and along the path you will see the playground below you on your left. Follow the path sloping up past the rhododendrons and take a sharp right: you walked down this path at the outset of the walk. You will find yourself once again on Fulwood Green with Fulwood Old Chapel ahead.

Further information:
Ball, Christine; Crossley, David; Flavell, Neville (2006). Water Power on the Sheffield Rivers: Second Edition. South Yorkshire Industrial History Society.
Forge Dam café: https://www.forgedamcafe.co.uk/our-story/
Friends of the Porter valley website: http://www.fopv.org.uk/Menu.htm
Sheffield Round Walk: http://theoutdoorcity.co.uk/sheffield-round-walk/
Shepherd Wheel: http://www.simt.co.uk/shepherd-wheel-workshop

Walk 9:   A walk around the Limb Valley

Introduction

This walk begins in the Porter Valley and climbs up through farmland to reach an area with magnificent views before descending into the Limb Valley to follow the course of the Limb brook upstream. After a possible stop off at a pub, the walk leads back into the Porter valley to return to its starting point.

Aside from the views, the Limb Valley provides a sense of peace and solitude where the only sounds are those of the birds and the trickling of water. Even though you are so close to the city, traffic cannot be heard and you and your dog can enjoy a sense of freedom gained from losing yourselves, (as opposed to being lost!), in this tranquil setting.

This walk follows a section of the Sheffield Round Walk which was created when local benefactor J.G. Graves worked with the council to secure the land for public use. As this is a walk of two valleys, there are a couple of steady up-hills and a couple of steep downhills. Your dog will appreciate the mixture of terrain as you cross woodland, streams and fields. Although there are no roads to concern you or your dog within the Limb Valley, you will pass through land where there may be livestock. There are waste bins situated at various points.

The Limb Brook rises in the village of Ringinglow, flowing east through Whirlow and Ecclesall Woods to join the River Sheaf. What is now a relatively insignificant waterway belies the fact that The Limb used to act as the boundary between the ancient kingdoms of Mercia and Northumbria, and later between Yorkshire and Derbyshire. This may account for its present name which could have evolved from forms of the word 'limit' (it has also been known as the 'Lymbrook' and the 'Fenny Brook'). Although this is now primarily an area of recreation for most people, the brook once provided the water power for corn and lead mills while tanning and coal mining took place along the route of this walk.

Limb Valley Route

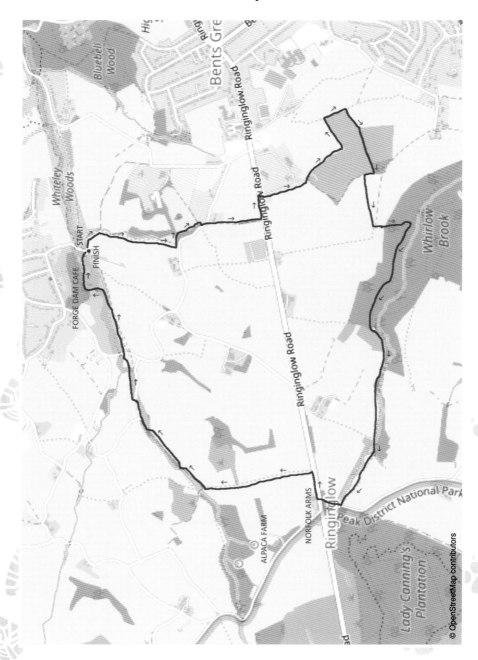

© OpenStreetMap contributors

Starting point:	Forge Dam: small parking area at very bottom of Brookhouse Hill
Location:	S10 4GN (nearest postcode); Grid reference: SK 30401 84949
Distance:	4 miles
Time:	2-3 hours

Directions:

From the car park at the bottom of Brookhouse Hill, take the second entrance on the left. This is the drive of Ivy Cottage Lane and at one time this was accessible to cars.

As you climb the path, on the right, note the steps leading to a small door set within the roots of a large tree. This 'fairy door' conceals some work put in place to help reinforce the base of the tree.

Continue a short way up Ivy Cottage Lane, past the house set back from the path, until you reach the stile on your right. The fields which lie to either side of the path may contain sheep.

In the eighteenth and nineteenth centuries, this was part of an area known as Whiteley Woods Village. Reminiscences collected by local historian Muriel Hall indicate that there was a lively little community here and it was considered to be the 'Queen of villages'. The Old School House set back from the path which you'll have just passed was a girls' school in the nineteenth century. Priest Hill Low Farm also stood near the lane whilst dotted around are Ivy Cottages, (known variously as 'Boulsover's Cottages', 'Wire Mill Cottages' and 'Whiteley Cottages'), Wire Mill Dam, the former Whiteley Wood Chapel and the site of Whiteley Wood Hall. These buildings, in addition to those at Forge Dam, are all connected with Thomas Boulsover who founded his Sheffield plate 'empire' in this area (see also **Walk 8**).

Cross over the stile to the right and follow the footpath which leads you up across fields in a south westerly direction. A few notes of caution here: there may be cows and considerable amounts of mud in these fields, depending on the season. Additionally, there are several stiles to negotiate which may prove challenging for larger dogs.

On the left, Sybrayhill Wood and a tributary to the Porter run along a small valley parallel with your path. To the right you'll see piles of large stones underneath copses, remnants, perhaps of buildings.

The steady climb up the field is rewarded with a panoramic vista. If you turn to face the the Mayfield Valley you may be able to identify the 'V' formation of three significant buildings: the former school house of David Lane Environmental Centre sits at the base of the 'V' while Bennet Grange and Fullwood Hall mark the left and right points respectively.

You may be aware of the sound of water as it trickles its way downstream through the fields to join the Porter below. Like the other walks in this guide, the role played by water in relation to the landscape is seen throughout this valley trail.

At the top of the field, exit via the solid stone steps in the wall and turn left onto Cottage Lane. Priest Hill Farm can be seen to the right.

Walk up the roadside for about 20 metres before dipping left in into a gap signposted 'Public Bridleway', (you will be following the bridleway for some distance). A Sheffield City Council sign indicates that you have arrived at 'Common Lane open space'. Cross the small brook as it curves up the edge of the field to the right. You can either take the same direction to follow the signposted 'Public Bridle Way' or head up the hill to the copse which affords a beautiful view across the Porter Valley. Your dog can run and chase about here, especially if you've brought a ball.

To rejoin the footpath, head down the field to the bottom left and meet another entrance to

Common Land. There are three attractive gateposts here and a treelined driveway.

Could this have been a driveway to Whiteley Wood Hall where Thomas Boulsover once lived? The main entrance was on Common Lane

Cross over the road, (which is Cottage Lane) and re-join the sign-posted bridleway situated up to the left from the footpath entrance. Waterways are temporarily left behind as the walk continues gently up the valleyside. More gateposts stand at the entrance from the road. One is fallen and the other is leaning rather precariously. Perhaps this is the result of an accident or an abandoned attempt to have them removed.

To the left of the path are the buildings of what was once Whiteley Wood Open Air School. It opened in 1909 so that children from around the city who were malnourished or debilitated by conditions such as asthma or tuberculosis could benefit from regular meals and fresh air. Their daily routine included time resting outside on deckchairs, as well as lessons outdoors. The school was in use until 1980.

Keep following the bridleway through the narrow avenue of trees, bordered with fields on the right (containing sheep, possibly).

Along the side of the pathway are two intriguing small, squared stone markers, both bearing the letters 'SEO' and 'EH'. These are old property boundary markers .

On your right there is grassed banking behind a long stone wall, underneath which lies a reservoir. At the end of the path, you'll emerge onto Ringinglow Road. This straight route was built in the eighteenth century and was a turnpike road leading from Sheffield into Derbyshire. Nowadays, some motorists take advantage of this straight route to speed out to the Peak District which lies just a few hundred metres to the west. The road is also popular with cyclists heading in the same direction. Turn left and to the east and walk along the roadside for about a hundred metres.

Emerging onto Ringinglow Road.

Cross the road to a wide entrance flanked by a large stone wall and continue to follow the signposted bridleway.

At the end of the driveway to your left lies Castle Dyke House which was formerly owned by the boxer Prince Naseem Hamed and a large tree provides information about model airplane flying times. Pass into the opening with Birkdale School's Brocksford Pavillion ahead of you. Follow the public footbath left which takes you through green metal gates. There's a waste bin situated next to the footpath opening.

This section of the walk features ever-changing views, thanks to its location on 'That great rise of land between Whirlow and Ringinglow Road', as described by local historian Roger Redfern. This is reflected in the name 'Whirlow' which indicates a place sited on a boundary mound. Whirlow, which lies just to the south, was once a village but is now an affluent suburb which retains its historic buildings in the form of traditional cottages and grand residences. The footpath passes close to Whirlow Hall Farm which is a thriving centre for school visits and events throughout the year.

Walk up the gently sloping path heading south, passing a walled copse of trees. The suburb of Bents Green is on your left to the east and you may be able to make out the long stone-tiled roof Thryft House, which dates back several hundred years. Views of south east Sheffield begin to open up and, as you climb, you may notice a breeze building.

Continue along this closely fenced path which skirts Birkdale School's playing fields. After a few minutes, the path bends round to the left and slopes slightly downwards towards the east. About five minutes later, you'll reach another gate. The footpath heads right and towards the south again before it opens out onto a public playing field. At this high point of the land, a stunning vista towards the east and the Sheaf valley to the south stretches out ahead. As you continue, the panorama widens to reveal landmarks such as Kepple's Column, Wincobank Hill, Sheffield College, Norton Water Tower and the tower blocks at Herdings which stick up like a couple of front teeth.

Continue south west along the pathway towards the Limb Valley then take up the bridle path heading right.

However, before taking the right turn, you may be interested in a diversion to the left which will lead you into a small plantation situated at the top of Coit Lane. This is used by educational groups visiting nearby Whirlow Hall Farm.

21st century open air school: the benefits for all children of learning outside are widely recognised.

Heading west.

The bridle path leads north out of this area and after about forty metres, climb over the wooden stile to your left. Your dog may be able to creep through the gap in the bottom of the gate.

Follow the path as it slopes up the edge of a field flanked to your left by a dry stone wall.

There are more views to be enjoyed up here, this time looking north to the ridge of Lodge Moor with

Loxley and Bradfield beyond. In the distance are the browns and ochres of moorland, contrasting with the gentle green slopes of the Mayfield Valley and the wooded Porter Valley. In the foreground, the different styles of pre and post-war suburban housing can be made out.

There is also a view of Sheffield's five valleys: to the north are the Porter, the Rivelin, and the Loxley. Towards the east and centre lies the wide, flat plain of the Don whilst the Sheaf is to the south.

At end of the field you will reach a stile to the left which can pose something of a challenge for dogs. It's worth being aware that there may be sheep in the fields ahead so negotiating the stile may allow you time to assess the situation before your dog does! Once you're on the narrow path, if you peep through the thicket of holly on the right, you may be able to make out a metal telephone mast which has been camouflaged so that it looks rather like a Christmas tree.

After a few metres, you'll reach the ridge at the top, with the two valleys of the Porter and the Limb lying on either side of you. This is known as the Bole Hill and it is a quiet and solitary spot. 'Bole' refers to the furnaces used in lead smelting which once took place here.
This exposed position on a windy hill helped to provide the conditions needed for the smelting process to take place. After lead smelting had ceased in this location, the landowners planted the slope with trees and went on to have stone walls constructed in order to enclose the land. Some of the dry stone walls we can see today are a testament to the toil and skill of local people from over two hundred years ago.

Progress through two beautifully constructed wooden stiles which are designed with dogs, as well as humans, in mind.

Ahead lies the Bole Hill plantation and the beginning of the descent towards the second valley of the walk.

Entering the plantation, the footpath takes you through the gap in the trees and down to a platform where there is a choice to be made.

The path to the right provides a gradual descent cutting diagonally through the plantation. This track has its challenges as it follows a narrow, steep and often muddy path. However, the hillside provides a quiet, still and dramatic land-scape. It also provides your dog with the opportunities to play 'fetch' up and down the slope.

You could instead take the very steep route which lies before you. This involves descending a stairway of one hundred and fifty-five steps (you may want to check this!). Fortunately, there is a hand rail to guide you down through this forest of imposing beech and larch while your dog can make its way freely. About three quarters of the way down, there is a memorial bench where you can pause to appreciate this woodland space which is carpeted in bluebells in the late spring. Around this point, you may be able to make out the sound of trickling water which means that the Limb Brook is not far away. The steps continue down to a track which meets the path.

The way back up: fortunately, this walk takes you down rather than up this path.

You've now joined the route of the Sheffield Round Walk and this will lead you to your starting point at Forge Dam. To the left, the Limb Brook continues on its down-ward course through Whirlow Park and into Ecclesall Woods.

This walk takes the opposite direction, and after your very steep descent, the footpath rises steadily towards the source of the Limb. The climb will be rewarded not only with splendid views but also with an opportunity for rest and refreshment for you both.

The neatly edged path runs between slopes wooded with huge beech and larch and then flattens out to reach a well-situated bench. Birch and pine trees can be seen rising to a great height on the opposite side of the valley. The Limb flows through a picturesque gorge which can be glimpsed through gaps in the wooded slopes. Birds such as chaffinches, wrens and tits flit around in the cover provided by these trees.

Whether you're progressing along the path or down the valley side, you'll be aware that the slope becomes very sheer. The enormous trees with their smooth silver-grey trunks stand solidly like so many pillars with their roots tightly grasping the soil.

To the left of the path, the terrain becomes mossy and marshy with little streams running down into the brook below. After about ten minutes, the valley side and valley bottom footpaths meet.

If you've taken the diagonal descent through the Bole Hill Plantation, you will emerge here to join the main footpath.

Continue over a small bridge. After rainfall, it seems that wherever you care to look, water is trickling and flowing down from the surrounding slopes and fields. You will then come upon a picnic bench sited within a flat, open area next to the Limb Brook. This is a lovely spot for a paddle as well as a picnic. Across the brook, there's a path which leads in a southerly direction up through the Rough Standhills plantation.

Your path continues on up the Limb Valley and through an area which has been known as Whirlow Glen. Now that the earlier stages of its course have been reached, the Limb is becoming so narrow that its banks could be leapt across easily.

Entering the glen.

There is a secluded and enchanted quality to this place. Everything seems to have been created on a small scale: the brook with its banks and waterfalls and the bridges which criss-cross its course. No wonder that, like Wyming Brook in **Walk 4**, this miniature valley has been called 'Little Switzerland.'

After about fifteen minutes, the final section of the Limb Valley walk is reached.

The gate leading into the final stage of the Limb Valley section of the walk

Cross the stile to the right and pass into an area of open farmland, reeds and sedges where there may be sheep or cattle. The vegetation indicates that this is a boggy area and the Limb Brook now runs some distance away to your right, picking up momentum as it begins its descent through its valley, part of which you have just walked.

Although it may be hard to imagine as you look across the marshy field, this area was once a scene of industry. Firstly, there is the ruined building

of Copperas House. Copperas was the name given to the chemical used in the tanning and dyeing process which was mined locally and processed here during the eighteenth and nineteenth centuries.

Old Copperas House: still just about standing.

The substance is toxic and was said to have a foul smell, yet people made their livings and their homes here over bygone centuries.

Local historian Shirley Frost provides a poignant account of an 'aged man' who worked alone here amidst the 'killing scent' during the 1830s.

On a foggy day in 2014 local artist Phlegm used a wall of the ruined Copperas House as the canvas for his painting of a Green Man.

Having passed Copperas House, Barber Fields lie in front of you. Shallow coal mining once took place beneath these fields, with an industrial rail track running nearby. Caving enthusiasts who investigated the mine in the 1950s reported that the tunnels were so close to the surface that it was possible to hear footsteps and voices above their heads!

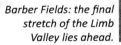

Barber Fields: the final stretch of the Limb Valley lies ahead.

Continue up the field to the stile in the stone wall and onto Sheephill Road.

You have reached the hamlet of Ringinglow. As with Whirlow, the suffix 'low' indicates that this was the site of a stone burial mound. Ahead of you is the building which was once Ringinglow Mission Chapel. Built in 1864, it did not attract many worshippers and by the 1930s it had ceased being used for its original purpose.

Take a right along the pavement to meet Ringinglow Road once again, but this time at a point further to the west than earlier in the walk. Across the road is the Roundhouse (which is actually octagonal). This is a former tollhouse dating from the later eighteenth century.

By this point you and your dog may feel that you have earned a visit to the Norfolk Arms pub.

A welcome sight for weary walkers

Whether you stop off here or not, from this point simply follow the directions leading from the Norfolk Arms in **Walk 7**. These will take you back down into the Porter Valley and to your starting point at the foot of Brookhouse Hill.

Further information:

Forge Dam Fairy Door Tree:
http://thetreehunter.tumblr.com/post/159827095924/
forge-dam-fairy-door-tree
Norfolk Arms: http://www.norfolkarms.com/
Sheffield Round Walk: http://theoutdoorcity.co.uk/sheffield-round-walk/
Sorby Natural History Society: http://www.sorby.org.uk/groups/
limb-valley-study-group/
Whirlow Hall Farm: http://www.whirlowhallfarm.org/

Walk 10:   A walk around Ecclesall Woods

Introduction

Ecclesall Woods is a great place for dog-walking. Within the extensive woodland (approximately 350 acres with over 15 km of public footpaths), dogs are able to run freely, explore and play. The woods are classed as ancient as they are documented as being in existence for at least four hundred years. During the Middle Ages the woods became part of a 'deer park' and were used primarily to ensure a steady supply of food and timber. From the sixteenth to the nineteenth century, the highly organised practice of coppicing took place as a means of supplying the wood for iron and lead smelting. Once grown and harvested, the timber was also processed in the woods and throughout this walk there are the traces of the 'Q-pits' where the 'white coal' used for lead smelting was produced. As with **Walks 7, 8** and **9**, the route also covers a section of the Sheffield Round Walk and we owe thanks to the entrepreneur and benefactor J. G. Graves, (1866-1945), for gifting this land to the people of Sheffield. If your dog enjoys water, the Limb Brook and its tributary the Ryecroft Brook run alongside woodland paths. The diverse joys of the woods are shared between walkers, bird-watchers, riders, joggers and cyclists. However, it's worth being aware that the woods are dissected by busy roads. It can be a surprise to hear roaring traffic and realise just how close these green and peaceful spaces lie to main roads running in and out of the city centre.

There is a special quality to a woodland walk. Although dog-walking can be a sociable activity for dogs and their owners, a saunter through the woods alone but for your canine companion can engender a sense of peace. Walking on the leafy woodland floor under the softening canopy of trees creates a soothing effect where it's possible to recharge and feel alive with our thoughts and with nature.

This 'special spell' created by the 'power of the wood' was highlighted by a journalist writing in the Sheffield Daily Telegraph at the beginning the last century. His article was entitled the 'Delights of Solitude in Ecclesall Woods' and in it he wrote that:

You get the sense of freedom which always seems to come as soon as one gets back to man's original home – the woods. The hum of traffic on the roads is lost. Nothing is heard but the birds and the faint buzz of insects... Such is the power of solitude in a wood. Such is the quiet, fascinating beauty of these lovely glades.

Thrush's 'anvil' at edge of Whirlow Playing Fields

Stone-balancing

'Fungus growing out of a tree'

The woods are a special place in which to engage with the natural world as each season unfolds. In the autumn, in addition to the stunning display of colour, there is a range of fungi to be seen. The winter is a good time for bird-watching and this walk skirts a bird sanctuary which was established in 1929. Nuthatches can be relatively easy to spot and to hear, (they seem particularly vocal little birds), with their pale blue plumage and black stripe running across their heads.

Another bird you're likely to see is the treecreeper. Both these birds spend their time foraging on tree trunks and branches; however, nuthatches tend to work their way downwards, whilst treecreepers move upwards.

Great spotted woodpeckers and jays are also common in the woods and if you hear a desolate and plaintive call, it could be from a buzzard whirling around slowly high above the treetops.

Ecclesall Woods is famed for its magnificent display of bluebells, but earlier in the spring, wood anemones spangle the woodland floor. The Woodland Discovery Centre provides information about the area and there are also information boards and signposts situated around the woods.

Woodland path through the bluebells

Wood anemones in April, making the most of the available sunlight before the tree canopy comes into leaf

As outlined earlier, Ecclesall Woods are divided into several sections by main roads. The walk detailed here takes place in Wood 3.
This section includes the Discovery Centre site and is bordered to the west by Ecclesall Road South, to the North by Abbey Lane and to the East by Abbeydale Road.

Ecclesall Woods Route

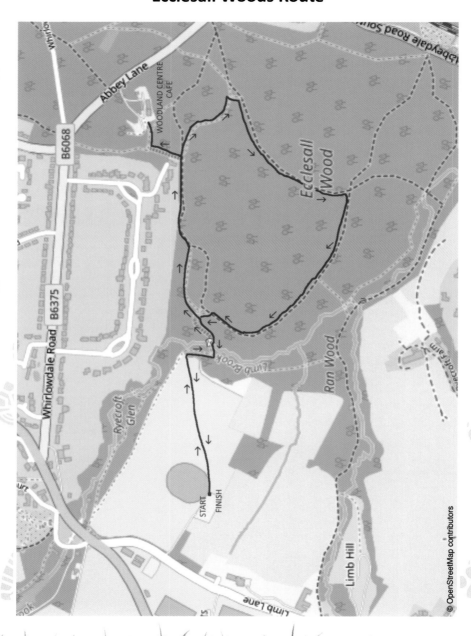

Starting point:	Whirlow Playing Fields car park off Limb Lane
Location:	S17 3ES (nearest postcode) Grid reference: SK 31126 82327
Distance:	Approx. 1½ miles
Time:	Approx. 1 hour

You could also base this walk from the J. G. Graves Woodland Discovery Centre missing out the Whirlow playing fields section, (although your dog may not thank you). The Woodland Discovery Centre provides a base for educational activities, local groups and events. There is an open-air café and water bowls for dogs are provided. There are toilets in the car park and within the Discovery Centre itself.

Dog-waste bins are provided at the car park on Limb Lane and at the Discovery Centre entrance to the woods

At certain times of year, there are sheep in the field adjoining the car park and the playing fields themselves are often used by children's football clubs at weekends.

Directions

Leaving the car park, head down towards the left hand corner of Whirlow Playing Fields in a diagonal direction. You may well encounter a great deal of mud at the top and bottom ends of the field. This is well-used by dog-walkers and so there's often a variety of hounds to be seen letting off steam, playing with each other and chasing after balls.

View across from the car park at Whirlow Playing Fields towards the woods; the colours of the grass, trees and sky are enhanced by the low sun of a late winter's afternoon.

When you reach the bottom corner of the field, you'll see an information board which provides a useful overview of the woods. Go through the small stile in the wall and enter woodland, with the Limb Brook running ahead of you. Pick your way over the exposed tree roots down to the bridge over the brook. After crossing the bridge, take a left and climb up the steps.

Footbridge over the Limb Brook

At the top of the steps, you have two options:

1) Stay left and enter the 'Donkey Field', (no donkeys). This little area, (more of a small, open, grassy space than a field), is a suntrap and there are benches where it's pleasant to sit and listen to the bullfinches which also seem to favour this spot. Moving on through the Donkey Field you'll find 'Donkey Field Pond' set back from the path. This has an information board and, if you're lucky, you may catch sight of dragonflies, a heron or even a fox having a drink.

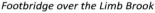

Donkey Field Pond: the heron's throat is bulging because it's in the process of swallowing a frog.

Leave the donkey field down through the gap next to the gate to re-join the main woods, walking down the slope and keeping to the left.

2) Take the path straight ahead of you

This will take you past the 'coin tree' on your right. After taking in this diversion, continue along the path which veers round to the left and down a slope to meet up with the path coming down from the Donkey Field gate.

Bluebell woods

The path you are now taking skirts the bird sanctuary, (which will be on your right throughout this part of the walk), in a clockwise direction. The bird sanctuary is enclosed as a haven for flora and fauna and, around this point, you will notice another fenced- off space to your right which has been partially cleared of trees to encourage a wild flower habitat.

Keep walking along the path until you reach the signposted turning for the The Woodland Coffee Stop on your left.

Refreshment opportunity?

Optional detour to Woodland Discovery Centre site

At this point you could take a detour left, follow the steps down and over the little bridge, take the path up and then follow the signposts pointing right to 'Sawmill' and 'Coffee Stop'. This leads you to the entrance to the Sawmill, Café and Discovery Centre site.

To re-join the walk, exit the site via the gate you came in by, turn right, follow the path down and over the bridge and then back up the steps to the Woodland Coffee Stop sign at the top. From here, you take up the main footpath again heading left.

Show me the way to the refreshments

Continuing on the walk around the perimeter of the bird sanctuary, follow the path round as it forks to the right and keep going ahead, over a flat bridge. Take the right hand turn and climb gently up a slope.

At the top of this, turn right and follow a wide path for a stretch. This path has the feel of a drive or an avenue. You will see on your left that there are a variety of species of trees such as beech, holly, sweet chestnut and oak. Many of them are mature specimens and have various forms of knotty and ridged bark distinctive of their species.

The fissured and twisted bark of an oak

The oak's canopy against a clear winter sky

Silver Birch bark

When you reach the end of this stretch of wide path, you will see ahead of you a kind of triangular coppice, with a sign-post. You could take any of these paths for lovely walks but for now follow the right fork, continuing your clockwise trail around the bird sanctuary. This is a gently curving uphill slope all the way to the next turn.

Further along this stretch of pathway on your left, there is an information board, explaining how the area was once used for a form of mining. As you proceed, you will notice wooden steps to your left. As the signpost indicates these lead down to the Limb Brook. Your path, however, continues in the sign-posted direction of 'Abbey Lane'.

If you look across from here into the bird sanctuary, you will see an area of

Which way?

tall conifers. From the late winter through the breeding season, these trees provide a nesting site for herons. The heronry makes for an enthralling sight which has been likened to a scene from the film Jurassic Park. If you're lucky, (and don't mind getting a crick in your neck), you'll be able to watch these rather reptilian-looking birds as they flap, clack and caw about in their precarious-looking nests and wheel around in the sky.

Heronry: the birds and their nests can be seen in the tree tops and branches

Further still up the path and on your left, you will come upon an open area created by the canopy of a magnificent beech, which is particularly stunning in the autumn. The beech may have a rope-swing attached to it and this, together with a bench nearby and a supply of sticks and squirrels would seem to ensure that all ages of dogs and humans are catered for in this delightful spot.

Bench in the beech clearing

Having a swinging time in May

Moving on up the incline, keep the wooded slopes of trees running down to Limb Brook on your left and the bird sanctuary on your right. Make your way up across the tree roots which are evident in an uneven but wide section of path.

Woodland path in autumn

At the 'corner' of this section, follow the path round to the right: there are more benches situated here which can provide glimpses of moorland and farmland views through the trees. After about 30m, the path slopes downwards and you should be able to make out ahead of you the green grass of the Donkey Field.

Walk towards this but, as you near the Donkey Field, take the fork left, down to the wooden steps which led you up here near the beginning of the walk. Follow the steps down and at the bottom, turn right onto the bridge across the Limb Brook. Walk up to the gap in the wall again and once through, you're back in Whirlow Playing fields. If your dog is still feeling energetic, here's a final opportunity for some ball action as you make your way up the field back to your car.

Further information:
Friends of Ecclesall Woods:
http://www.friendsofecclesallwoods.org.uk/about/WoodlandHistory/
J. G. Graves Woodland Discovery Centre:
http://www.wildsheffield.com/woodland-discovery-centre
Sheffield Round Walk: http://theoutdoorcity.co.uk/sheffield-round-walk/
RSPB Bird Identifier:
https://www.rspb.org.uk/birds-and-wildlife/wildlife-guides/bird-a-z/

Bibliography

Ball, C., Crossley D. & Flavell, N. (2006). *Water Power on the Sheffield Rivers.* 2nd ed., Wakefield, South Yorkshire Industrial History Society.

Davey, S. R. (no date). *"Where t'watter runs o'er t'weir". A look back at Sheffield's Watermills. Sheffield,* Parker Press.

Frost, S. (1990). *Whirlow. The story of an ancient Sheffield hamlet.* Sheffield, J.W. Northend Ltd.

Hall, M. (1974). *More About Mayfield Valley and Old Fulwood.* Sheffield, J.W.Northend Ltd.

Haythornthwaite, G. (1984). *The Story of Sheffield's Green Belt and a Guide to its Future by CPRE.* South Yorkshire Printers.

Hey, D. (1980). *Packmen, Carriers and Packhorse Roads. Trade and Communications in North Derbyshire and South Yorkshire.* Leicester University Press.

Hey, D. (2010). *A History of Sheffield. 3rd ed.,* Lancaster, Carnegie Publishing Ltd.

Hindmarch, D. (2005). *Sheffield Parks and Gardens.* Stroud, Tempus Publishing.

Hunter, J. (1819). *Hallamshire: The History and Topography of the Parish of Sheffield. 3rd ed.,* London, Virtue & Company Ltd. Edited with prefaces and additions to text by Gatty, A. (1875).

Jones, M. (1989). *Sheffield's Woodland Heritage*. Sheffield, Sheffield City Libraries.

Jones, M. (2004). *The Making of Sheffield*. Barnsley, Wharncliffe Books.

Machan, P. (1975). *Water Mills of the River Sheaf – A Survey of What Remains.* Sheffield, P. Machan.

Pawson, H. & Brailsford, J. (1862). *Pawson and Brailsford's Illustrated Guide to Sheffield and Neighbourhood. 2nd ed*. (1985). Republished with foreword by Mary Walton (1971). Otley, The Amethyst Press.

Redfern, R. (1998). *Sheffield's Rural Fringe.* Old Brampton, The Cottage Press.

Shaw, S. & Kendall, K. (2015). *Walking the Rivelin: A Pocket Guide to the industrial heritage and natural history of the Rivelin Valley. 5th ed.*, Sheffield, Arc Publishing & Print.

Walton, M. (1968). *Sheffield and its Achievements. 4th ed.*, Wakefield, S.R. Publishers Ltd.

Other local titles available from Arc Publishing

Sheffield Past, Places and People

A wonderful collection of photographs from Sheffield's past. The book has a section dedicated to the 1950s, 60s and 70s plus a great set of pictures from 1900 into the 1940s. Also included are photographs of the old Sheffield markets and some of the destruction Hitler caused during the Blitz.

Most photos have Sheffield people featured in them, so you never know; you might see someone you recognise! **£10.99**

A Photographic Journey down Ecclesall Road

This is an informative enjoyable photographic record of Ecclesall Road. Its rich diversity is well covered and brings back happy memories travelling along one of Sheffield's finest roads. This A4 landscape book not only has many photos from the early 19th century but some as late as the 1980s. It is lovely to be able to follow the route from Whirlow - seeing the changes along the way to the city centre. **£11.99**

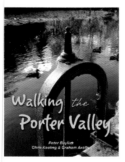

Walking the Porter Valley

The book is a journey up the Porter Valley, looking at the flora, birds, geology and history of a much loved and used area of outstanding beauty in Sheffield. Follow the River Porter from Hunter's Bar to its source on the moors, near Rud Hill, high above the west of Sheffield. It combines a walking guide with a wealth of information about the Porter Valley. It is richly-illustrated with old photographs and information showing what the valley was like in the past. **£8.99**

Sheffield 10

Photographic memories of Broomhill, Crookes and many other suburbs of S10.
A fascinating look back in time.
£8.99

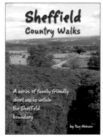

Sheffield Country Walks

24 walks around many of the city's suburbs enjoying stunning views and interesting landmarks.
£7.99

Visit our website: www.sheffieldbooks.co.uk

**AVAILABLE FROM MOST GOOD BOOK SHOPS OR DIRECT FROM ARC PUBLISHING
TELEPHONE ORDER LINE: 07809 172872**